The Guiding Purpose Strategy

A Navigational Code for Brand Growth

Markus Kramer
with Tofig Husein-zadeh

Clink
Street

London | New York

Acknowledgements

My deepest thanks to all of you who contributed through sharp, insightful and forward-looking thinking. I am most grateful for the countless encounters both personally and professionally with so many great brand builders, leaders and people without whom the accumulated experience that led to *The Guiding Purpose Strategy* could never have been achieved. You are generous and kind, in all corners of the world - and you are simply too many to list here – but you know who you are. Many thanks to my business partner, Reto Zangerl, at Brand Affairs. Without his perspective, flexibility and time, this project would never have seen the light. A warm thank-you to my co-author Tofig Husein-zadeh for his focus, wisdom and unwavering dedication to help me write this navigational map for which no blueprint existed until our kick off on a mountain top in 2015. Thank you, Angela M. Harp for keeping me on my toes by challenging the thinking and honing the structure and language aspects of this work. And thank you, Gareth Howard and Hayley Radford of Authoright for your expert advice and fabulous support in getting this to the finish line. But most of all, thanks to my beloved family – you are the source of my energy and my passion for life.

Markus Kramer

*Dedicated to those who get that
it's never just business.*

"Profit for a company is like oxygen for a person. If you don't have enough of it, you're out of the game. But if you think your life is about breathing, you're really missing something..."

Prof. Peter Ferdinand Drucker
Austrian-born American
Author, Consultant and
Father of Modern Management
(1909–2005)

A note on the Coat of Arms

The Guiding Purpose Strategy

The North Star on the upper left-hand corner of the shield symbolizes the importance of guidance and progress on one's life journey. It carries archetypal power and a deep meaning that transcends culture, ethnicity, religion and geographical location.

The compass refers to one's current orientation. One who is fully aware of their whereabouts at any given point in time is in a position to map the route, make the necessary decisions and set the path destined for a better place.

The pocket watch reminds us how time is a part of a grand equation and how little time we have to make a real difference. The symbol of the timepiece emphasizes the longitudinal knowledge that withstands the test of time.

The ship's wheel represents the vital role of becoming a leader and taking control. It stands for self-leadership, the drive to lead in thought, in an organization and in one's own field or market.

In its entirety, the shield protects that which is worth preserving. It gives balance to the concentrated power of each of the key symbols with which it has been mindfully adorned. If the symbols collectively communicate positive progress, the shield then communicates protection and preservation – all is connected, operating as one.

Contents

INITIATION 1

Welcome 3
Eliminating Low Definitions 7
From Cartography to GPS 11

FEW TO ALL. ALL TO ALL. 17

Everywhere and Nowhere 19
We Are On Air 23
Multiple Personality Order 27
The Opinion Economy 31
The Viral Spiral 37

PURPOSE PERSPECTIVES 43

Don't Hide Behind the Brand 45
Signs From the Future 49
Reducing Pain and Maximizing Pleasure 53
The Blue Genie Effect 57
Heroes, Giants, Gods 61
Transformation of Value Chains 65
The Supreme Network 71
Slow Death 77

ON PURPOSE 81

Essence and Appearance 83
Hidden P's of Marketing 85
The Shaman and the Meaningful Brand 87
The Guiding Purpose 89
How Luxury Brands Apply Purpose 93
The Changing Nature of Consumers 99

GPS - GUIDING PURPOSE STRATEGY 105

Decoding and Assembling Purpose 107
The GPS Framework 111
Seeking and Finding Purpose 117
Articulating and Clarifying Purpose 121
Shared and Aligned Purpose 127
Measuring Purpose 133

APPLYING PURPOSE 139

Start Focusing and Stop Copying 141
Taking 3rd Place 145
On the Test of Time 147
Leadership and Organizational Culture 149
How Purpose Propels Growth 153

MAKING IT HAPPEN 157

Conquering Time 159
Productivity Mantra 165
Branding Thyself 169
Cultivating the Culture of the Self 173
The Future of Personal Mastery 175
The Last Word 177

Initiation

Welcome

"The only constant is change."

Heraclitus of Ephesus (c. 535 BC–475 BC)
Greek Philosopher who believed
change was central to the universe

The very fact you are reading these lines may indicate that you are one of the select few intent on making change happen. We cannot define your reasoning, but we can confidently say that we will provide you with an *all-Purpose tool* to master your journey towards change. Think of it as a Swiss army knife of some sort – beautiful, simple, effective and easy to use. Once you learn how to use it, you will find it convenient to carry with you wherever you go. But beware: it is not a toy and it will require a little time and patience to learn how to craft with it.

We believe that the coming era will be one of radical transparency. For businesses, brands and their leaders, the implications are powerful, albeit not exactly obvious. So, what is it going to take to create thriving value propositions, products, and services, and indeed anchor ourselves in this new post-positioning period of total connectedness?

As societies mature, economic development accelerates, and competitive pressure continues to increase, our individual and collective craving for orientation is on the rise. A statistical analysis of text content over the last two centuries supports this notion. Google Books Ngram Viewer analyzes the vast content of millions of books and outputs a graph that represents and contrasts the use of a particular term throughout time.

Figure 1: Google Ngram on Leadership and Strategy

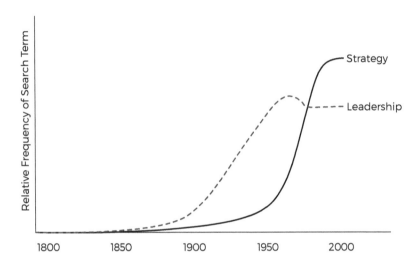

Note the steep climb of 'Strategy' entering into our vocabulary. Strategy intertwined with leadership takes us to a desired future. For example, achieving a personal objective or reaching targets in business. However, we claim that neither will be enough to master the future successfully. We see Purpose as the North Star providing guidance and direction. We are not suggesting that Leadership or Strategy will become less important, but rather that these critical areas will need to be boosted by adding meaning to whatever you do in order to become or stay successful in the future.

One thing is clear – a meaningful brand driven by a higher Purpose drives profits. Purposeful brands outperform the stock market by 133%, gain 46% more share of wallet and achieve marketing results that are double those of lower rated brands.[1] But real Purpose goes beyond profit and certainly beyond 'Corporate Social Responsibility' and all the fancy reports that brush over

---

1   Smith, Shaun. "Customer Experience: On Purpose." *Brand Quarterly.* 30 Sept. 2016.
<http://www.brandquarterly.com/customer-experience-on-purpose.>

the underlying, often systemic issues. Business models properly centered on Purpose build beneficial relationships with external stakeholders and drive culture from within. A sense of real Purpose has numerous positive effects. Perhaps most importantly, it has a major impact on job satisfaction.[2]

The Guiding Purpose Strategy is in many ways a reflection of our society. In writing this book, it was certainly invaluable to put it up against a new industrial context where the convergence of attitudes and consumption behavior among younger generations can be seen through a different lens. *The Guiding Purpose Strategy* – in short *GPS* – is an instrument to discover Purpose, the main ingredient needed to create and sustain a meaningful brand, a company or indeed a life. It provides a transferable methodology that promises to increase returns and improve results, both literally and intrinsically.

Building on many years of experience in working with some of the most inspiring brands in the world, from consumer products to government institutions to charities and tech startups, we demonstrate how the application of the *GPS Framework* can help create value systems that lead to prosperity at both an organizational and an individual level. We pay particular attention to the luxury sector, an industry in which passion and Purpose-driven brands have stood the test of time.

For the underpinning explorations of this book to be fruitful, we thought it best to remain open for serendipitous possibilities. One never knows from whom or from where the next big thing might come. So instead of limiting ourselves to the 'business' or 'social science' shelves, we also looked in the most unexpected places. We spoke with younger and older generations, leaders, entrepreneurs, brand experts and many others. Our research had to go beyond the heap of traditional management material. It also had to be multilingual, taking into account large amounts of data not yet translated into English. As authors of different cultural backgrounds and generations, we took advantage of the opportunity to combine our worlds of Eastern wisdom and Western constructivism. To enrich our minds even further, we referenced various works of enlightenment, drawing knowledge from a range of sources, including Greek philosophers to more recent marketing case studies, academic lectures and scholarly articles.

---

2 Job Satisfaction Index 2015. Happiness Research Institute. Krifa. TNS Gallup

As we believe intellectuals have done enough dividing and too little assembling, we were intent on taking an interdisciplinary approach. That is to say, we followed the old alchemical maxim *solve et coagula*, which means to dissolve and coagulate, analyze and synthesize. Our interdisciplinary take on Purpose involves examining across and in between fields, cultures, relationships, etc. As Rory Sutherland, Vice-Chairman of Ogilvy Group UK, so eloquently put it: "… the most interesting thing that's happening in any field is not in any field, it's actually in the interplay between different fields." The key advantage of an interdisciplinary approach is that if the solution cannot be found within one field, it is to be found in another.

It is the individuals and companies with clarity of Purpose that are changing the world, bit by bit. Leaders, marketers, entrepreneurs and professionals who understand the power of inner Purpose are destined to become the positive change-makers of tomorrow.

Our intention is to pass on the *spirit and mindset* with which *The Guiding Purpose Strategy* book was written. So, if you are looking for a typical step-by-step strategy book, you might be better off looking elsewhere. If you're up for a journey towards professional and personal growth – we are excited to have you on board!

Eliminating Low Definitions

*"Analgesics that are branded are more effective at reducing pain
than analgesics that are not branded.
I don't just mean through reported pain reduction,
but actual measured pain reduction."*

Rory Sutherland
Perspective is Everything
TED conference

A concept central to this book is the notion of 'brand,' regardless of whether you are reading this for business or personal growth – or both. Essentially, brand value is the ultimate currency companies, and increasingly more individuals crave. Sir John Hegarty, co-founder of BBH and one of the world's most awarded ad men said it best: "Don't start a business, build a brand."[3]

But as long as we keep describing the notion of 'a brand' in a confusing way, we will continue to have a vague understanding of it. So, let's start by defining what a brand is. A brand differentiates something or someone from its competition and instills trust, simplifies choice by reducing risk, spurs demand and creates

---

3   Lepitak, Stephen. "Don't Start a Business, Build a Brand: Sir John Hegarty on Working in the Startup Sector." *The Drum.* 02 May 2017. <http://www.thedrum.com/news/2017/05/02/dont-start-business-build-brand-sir-john-hegarty-working-the-startup-sector>.

pricing power and – all being well – builds loyalty and creates value over time. At the time of writing, the most valuable brand in the world is Apple, with a whopping US$170 billion in brand worth.[4] Clearly, when things are done right, brands manage to create tremendous amounts of economic value. We can derive from his that 'brand' is something hugely valuable, yet miraculously intangible.

You might not become the next Apple, but there is still a lot to learn from the concept of brand. In early Egypt, Rome and Greece, for instance, merchants painted their storefronts and hung pictorial signs to communicate what goods they had on offer to a mostly illiterate population. Historically, branding mostly meant stamping things. In other words, this was about claiming objects by putting your name or your mark on it. Cowboys would brand their cows, hence our modern term 'brand' or 'branding,' which derives from the iron rod used to 'brand' an animal. This helped cattlemen collect their livestock at the end of the day from the vast prairies. It also made it easier for them to sell their cattle. A good 'brand' on an animal could be trusted. And trust equaled money.

Branding endows products and services with the power of the brand.

In medieval times and later during the Renaissance and the Enlightenment, prominent architects and stonemasons who belonged to a certain guild would leave symbols on the monumental cathedrals and palaces they built in hope of being recognized by other guild members for their efforts.

Today, branding is still about leaving a mark. But as competition increases, so too does the effort of marketers to stand out. The consequences? Brands are being associated with promises that are increasingly hard to fulfill. Havas Media's 'Meaningful Brands' study shows that consumers wouldn't even care, let alone feel the difference if almost 70% of existing brands disappeared from the face of the earth.[5]

It is also easy to assume that 'being a brand' equates to simply being a big company – like Apple. But remember, even Apple started humbly. Cameron Craig, a communications professional, who did PR for Apple for ten years, learned from his journey that brand is a valuable asset: "Most importantly,

4   http://interbrand.com/best-brands/best-global-brands/2016/ranking/apple/ accessed 18 July 2017
5   Meaningful Brands Powered by Havas. N.p., n.d. Web. <http://www.meaningful-brands.com/en>.

respect your brand. That's the biggest lesson of all that I learned at Apple. It's your biggest asset and you have to protect it." Indeed, people come and go. Brands, if managed carefully over time, remain top of mind with consumers far longer than employees stay with a company.

As we progress on our journey towards finding, articulating and harnessing the idea of a strongly rooted Purpose, we must learn about the intricacies of differentiating, positioning, creating a unique value proposition and building a loyal audience through the power of brand. But where should we look? There are certainly many lessons to learn from the dazzling world of luxury than you may think. But first things first: anyone navigating towards a substantially better future requires a map to get there.

From Cartography to GPS

"The real voyage of discovery consists not in seeking new landscapes but in having new eyes."

Marcel Proust
French Novelist

Regardless whether you're a firm, a brand, or an individual, you definitely need to implement specific strategies to grow, to thrive and to achieve permanent success. The science and art of such stratagem is based on orientation. In order to thrive, you first need to know exactly where you are. This means being totally honest with yourself about where you currently stand and how solid your stance is. It is important to know where you want to end up – even down to the exact address of your final destination. The instrument that allows you to pinpoint a desired destination is also the instrument that will take you there.

So, in general, Strategy, with a capital S, is more about navigation and exploration rather than war or battle. You cannot be a war general if you don't know how to navigate. Understanding the role of maps and having a good sense of direction has always been essential for leaders and entrepreneurs across industries and throughout history in order to conquer and win in their fields. Let's travel through time and refresh our memories on the history of mankind's relationship with cartography.

Merriam Webster's Dictionary[6] defines cartography as:

1. The process or skill to draw maps
2. The science or art of making maps

It is worth noting that the earliest known maps were of the heavens, not of the earth. The earliest cartographers were also the first experts in geometry and astronomy. As masters of calculation, they were called on to consult the kings and pharaohs in ancient times.

Buckminster Fuller, the futurologist who was awarded the Royal Gold Medal for Architecture, writes about a successful group of mapmakers and explorers in his book, *The World Man*. Fuller describes such worldly men as being extraordinary at designing vessels and carrying out expeditions in a strategic manner: "They had high proficiency in dealing with celestial navigation, the storms, the sea, the men, the ship, economics, biology, geography, history, and science. The wider and more long-distanced their anticipatory strategy, the more successful they became." These World Men were especially triumphant during the Age of Exploration, also known as the Age of Discovery. They were the great adventurers, mapmakers and seafarers who operated globally. Through their processes of experimentation, measuring and inventing, they inevitably developed fortune-producing enterprises.

It is due to the adventurous spirit of history's brave explorers that the North Star became the functional anchor for orientation. World explorers, excursionists, travelers and voyagers passed through boundless deserts guided by its light. The North Star is constant and reliable in an ever-changing, unpredictable world.

In the time of Ferdinand and Isabella as well as other maritime monarchs, maps were top-secret.[7] But it was not just about mapping geographic territory or destination points. Some began mapping in other fields like architecture and biology, too. The wayfarers, the architect- and sculptor-guilds who planted the first seeds of the Renaissance were also aware of the beneficial functions of map-making. Likewise, botanists and zoologists saw the value

---

6 "Cartography." Merriam-Webster, <http://www.merriam-webster.com/dictionary/cartography>.
7 McLuhan, Marshall. *Understanding Media*. London: Sphere, 1973. .

of mapping plants and animals. Mapping the human anatomy, however, remained taboo for quite some time. In fact, it was prohibited up until 1315 when Mondino de Luzzi, an Italian surgeon, published *Anatomia*, the first manual and map on dissection.

Map-making was also an integral part of various firms, although not commonly known outside the business world. Merchants and entrepreneurs often took advantage of travelers with business acumen for their cartographic skills in trading processes or building an enterprise. Maps helped increase efficiency, as decisions could be made based on measurement and analysis, while operations could be simplified and workflows documented. Ultimately, maps served as guidance and direction in stratagem. Cartography was instrumental in turning management into a science, as business process mapping started to demystify the complexities of an organization. A business process map allows for alignment on what best route to take in order to make improvements to a particular process, perhaps increasing efficiency, delivering a product quicker or making customer experience better.

Nonetheless, the idea of business maps – namely, detailed diagrams of a company's operations and workflows – did not reach their heights until the beginning of the 20th century. For example, Allan H. Mogensen, an American industrial engineer and authority in the field of work simplification began training business people in the 1930s in map-making. One of his students, Art Spinanger used his newly acquired business map-making skills to help Procter & Gamble streamline its operations.

With the invention of electric and digital technologies came the revolution of cartography. Maps could now be regularly and instantly updated, which greatly improved their accuracy. Towards the end of the 20th century humanity found ways to create a genetic map. The completion of genome mapping will certainly be a critical turning point, not just in the history of cartography. "Like the system of interstate highways spanning our country, the map of the human genome will be completed stretch by stretch," says James Watson, the Nobel Prize Laureate and co-discoverer of the structure of

DNA.[8] Map-making has taken us from navigating land and sea, to mapping history, understanding business processes and even decoding our own origins. It seems only natural that the concept of the North Star can serve us well in outlining a *Guiding Purpose Strategy*.

We've definitely come a long way since de Luzzi's original maps of the anatomy. Cartography of the body has evolved to a point where scientists have constructed a map of the brain and can identify which parts of the brain react to specific images, sounds or situations, thanks to technologies such as electroencephalography (EEG) or functional magnetic resonance imaging (fMRI). These types of development made way for today's prospering field of neuromarketing. Marketers began measuring various product-related characteristics such as the crunchy sounds of potato chip packaging in order to identify what types of tonality ignites signals of arousal in the brain of the consumer when touching the packaged good. Most neuromarketing experts agree on the fact that the importance of visual storytelling in brand communications cannot be overstated. Indeed, storytelling began with the shamans of ancient cultures. And neuroscience has shown that the ancient skill of storytelling and creating narratives of legends and myths is a pastime that is not only still very much alive – it prevails.

May Britt-Moser and Edvard I. Moser were awarded the 2014 Nobel Prize in Physiology or Medicine for their discovery of cells that constitute a positioning system in the brain. They claimed to have discovered "an 'inner GPS' in the brain that makes it possible to orient ourselves in space, demonstrating a cellular basis for higher cognitive function."[9] Thanks to our inner GPS, we know where we are, and we know how we are able to find our way from one place to another. Essentially, we store information in such a way that we can immediately trace our steps the next time we take the same path.

If we were to travel back a century, we would see that secret intelligence service agencies had the first Global Positioning System. Its invention changed everything, operating in real time, which saved huge amounts of time in reaching target points during investigations. For a long time, a GPS was just

---

8   Watson, James D. and Norton Zinder. "Genome Project Maps Paths of Diseases and Drugs." *New York Times*. The New York Times, 12 Oct. 1990. <http://www.nytimes.com/1990/10/13/opinion/l-genome-project-maps-paths-of-diseases-and-drugs-239090.html>.
9   ibid.

an idea explored in Hollywood movies. Today, if you have a smartphone in your pocket a GPS is always with you.

The Global Positioning System is an indication of how we have successfully mapped the *outer* world – its nautical and aeronautical maps help us orientate and navigate our way around. However, we are still missing a key kind of a navigational instrument to guide us inwardly. If companies, leaders, brands and entrepreneurs are to secure their future, they must create a map of their *inner* worlds. Historically, we began by mapping the heavens, then the world around us. Now, it's time to take what we have inherited from a long history of cartographers a step further and create a map that leads us to our inner North Star. Just think of it as a new dimension of the GPS, one that points us in the direction of what makes us thrive. According to research from Jonathan Trevor, Associate Professor of Management Practice at Saïd Business School, University of Oxford, the key to creating and sustaining a winning organization is to ensure the company is strategically aligned – arranging all elements of an organization to optimally support the fulfillment of its long-term Purpose.[10]

We live in times of unprecedented change, which requires us to connect and think beyond the parameters of the GPS we know today. If you have come this far, you have just discovered our rationale for calling this new inner, guiding instrument *The Guiding Purpose Strategy*, a.k.a. *GPS*.

10 Trevor, Jonathan. "News." *Saïd Business School.* University of Oxford, 20 May 2016. <http://www.sbs.ox.ac.uk/school/news/best-companies-are-best-aligned?utm_source=Twitter&utm_medium=link&utm_campaign=Corporate_JonathanTrevorHandles_JUN16>.

Few to all.
All to all.

Everywhere and Nowhere

"We are moving towards a new kind of augmented intelligence, defined by harnessing decision support systems and ambient computing that can support humans to solve problems individually and collectively that were previously beyond our capacity."

Sir Nigel Richard Shadbolt
Professor of Artificial Intelligence
University of Southampton

Technology that is everywhere all the time becomes invisible at some point. Mark D. Weiser, former chief scientist at Xerox said: "The most profound technologies are those that disappear. They weave themselves into the fabric of everyday life until they are indistinguishable from it." For the very first human beings on our planet, language was high technology but as time passed it became part of everyday life – invisible like oxygen, yet vital for survival. Similarly, electricity was once a luxury of the few, today it is everywhere and nowhere. Now, it is digital media that is omnipresent.

The fact that digital media is omnipresent in our lives has a much to do with our physical environment. We were first introduced to Newtonian physics before we began exploring quantum physics. In the 21st century we are transitioning to the physics of information – a world that presents both challenges and opportunities we have yet to fully comprehend. When we talk about the physics of information, we essentially mean the laws underpinning the very notion of this transition. For instance, the omnipresence of hyperconnected digital media, enabled through fiber optics and free and superfast Wi-Fi, is a direct characteristic of what we would term the physics of information. According to Jay Walker-Smith at Yankelovich Consumer Research, we've gone from being exposed to about 500 ads a day back in the 1970s to as many as 5000 a day today.[11] It's almost overwhelming to consider the speed of this new physical reality. Nowadays, most things we do digitally are at the speed of light. It's a conundrum of sorts. We live in a fast, super-connected, and supposedly super-efficient world, but somehow we still don't have time for anything. It is as if we are wasting more time to save time. As Tom Ford, the American designer and film director, stated: "Time and silence are the most luxurious things today."

There are more distractions than ever, more ways to be interrupted from whatever it is we're doing – a vibrating smartphone in your pocket, a loud TV commercial, a popup ad on your browser, an animated billboard on the street, nonstop Whatsapp or Snapchat pings that you simply can't ignore. Where does it end? In order to retain focus and keep balanced as human beings, but also as brands or businesses, we must develop critical skills to master our lives in this regard. Developing an optimum differentiation system is a way to improve the decision-making processes in times of information overload. It seems a necessity to develop an index, a tool that helps us navigate through the new reality we live in today. It's key function: to cut through the clutter of choice and information that saturates our lives.

Historically speaking, knowledge was accessible only to the elite few and not yet democratized the way it is today. Yet people always raised plenty of questions, which often led to revolutions. The fundamental issue was that people couldn't find answers to their questions. Today, however, not having answers is rare. The issue is more about asking the right question than finding the correct answer in the clutter of information. It was the modernist poet T.S. Eliot who pondered this issue even before the age of digitalism: "Where is the wisdom we have lost in knowledge? Where is the knowledge we have

---

11 Johnson, Caitlin. "Cutting Through Advertising Clutter." CBS News. CBS Interactive, 17 Sept. 2006. <http://www.cbsnews.com/news/cutting-through-advertising-clutter/> accessed 6 October 2017

lost in information?" It is as if we are drowning in information for craving knowledge. The hierarchy between information, knowledge and intelligence is illustrated in Figure 2, with intelligence being the least in quantity and the highest value in quality. In this kind of environment, it is not those who have access to knowledge who will win, but those who gather the intelligence to develop their own informational navigation index.

Figure 2: The new Know-How is the new Know-Why
(from information to intelligence)

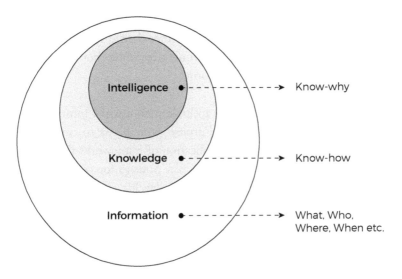

In an interview, communications analyst Marshall McLuhan explained: "There is in IBM, for example, a phrase: 'information overload produces pattern recognition' [...] When you give people too much information they instantly resort to pattern recognition." It is not to say that this giant quantum leap forward of media and technology is wrong or right. Making value judgments when analyzing such grand shifts in civilization is not a pragmatic practice. Besides, it is too early for that. It is always smarter to simply stand back, break the paradigm into several parts and analyze it as systematically as possible in order to have a better view of the real zeitgeist of our times. There's no point in strategizing unless it is fully acknowledged that this present paradigmatic situation does, in fact, exist. To quote Don Draper from *Mad Men*: "Change is not good or bad. It just is."

The more choice there is, the more difficult it is to decide. Aiming for clarity and cutting through the clutter is therefore a key skill to master in the 21st century. But it's harder than it sounds. It takes time to master and if your selection process is not underpinned by sound judgment, then the outcome of your decision will likely be suboptimal. So, how then do we optimize our choices?

To enhance our ability to make the right choice, whether personal or professional, we need to develop and embed a sort of automatism, an instinct for the right thing to do in any given situation.

The guiding Purpose principle is a mind's eye that allows you to keep your head above the flow of information rather than drown in it. Properly developed, it will yield clarity, help save time, streamline choices and increase the likelihood of making optimal decisions.

We'll use the subsequent chapters to look at contextual information and explore why the idea of a guiding Purpose principle is so central to our thinking, before moving on to the application of frameworks that will allow you to access the power of a *Guiding Purpose Strategy* for yourself and your brand. The ultimate goal is to help you to develop your very own inner compass to navigate the future successfully.

We Are On Air

"The question isn't: 'What do we want to know about people?'
It's: 'What do people want to tell about themselves?'"

Mark Zuckerberg
Entrepreneur, Founder of Facebook

R&R Partners is probably best remembered for creating the campaign slogan 'What Happens in Vegas, Stays in Vegas.' A brilliant positioning claim that states that whatever happens during your visit, only happens there. And it happens far enough away not to have any negative effect on the 'the here and now.'

Anyone born after 1985 and before 2005 is loosely termed a Millennial. Anyone born after 2005 will most likely fall into the category of Generation Z – a demographic that has yet to arrive into working life. Generational theory suggests significant changes across these bands (such as perspective on life, the attitude towards spending, belief and value systems etc.). However, it is most certainly the area of communication that leads to fundamental change in how we live. Up to Generation X (born after 1970 and before 1985), people mostly had one reality to contend with: *off the record*. The rapid evolution of technology has led to unprecedented change in how we communicate. Today, we essentially live in three different realities: *on the record*, *off the record* and a balanced blend of both, or what we will call an *amalgam* reality. Millennials and generations after them already live in these three realities simultaneously.

The idea of being *on the record* has always existed. This is Vegas and anything happening there right now. However, the *on the record* reality used to be a mere representation or rather a piece of the *off the record* reality. It used to be just something that was recorded. Someone would say, "We are on air," which quite literally would refer to 'we are now being recorded' – a not so typical occasion. One would pay attention to what, how and where things would be 'recorded.' Fast forward several paradigm shifts within the media and technology landscape and the *on the record* reality has broadened its meaning to include an entire world. It is now a dimension by itself and it is as big, if not bigger, than the *off the record* world.

We are witnessing the creation of a new normal in business culture, on an individual level and on a general sociocultural level, too. Anyone with teenage children will easily relate to how profound this shift is, but accepting it as a new normality is even tougher. For many, being *off the record* feels dangerously uncomfortable as it implies being left out of the conversation. There are very few users of social media who use Facebook, Snapchat, Instagram and the like because they have something to say. The large majority of social media users are actively using it because they feel they *have to* say something.

One may argue, the bigger the media-tech world, the smaller the *off the record* reality. It is useful to bear in mind though that one of the major differences between the contents of the two is that the *on the record* is much more linear than the *off the record* world. *On the record* depends on language (visual or verbal) whereas *off the record* relies more on human consciousness.

It is essential to emphasize how dangerously easy it is today to be *on the record*. Simply by pulling a smartphone out of your pocket and tapping the screen with your finger, you are on air and *on the record*, most likely forever. This unprecedented ease of being *on the record* whenever, wherever, and whoever you are, has become one of the major driving forces of change in modern society. Anyone living in a democratic society has a voice, but to be *on the record* in a matter of seconds and at your will is beyond just having your voice heard. From a macroeconomic perspective, the communicative power has shifted to the consumer in an unparalleled way. This changes everything for brands, global organizations and firms, governments, authorities and so on.

There can be no doubt that this shift in how we live and perceive reality will lead to a much more fragmented, much more complex – but as we shall see later on, also a much more transparent – world. Therefore we need to dig up the relevant contextual drivers to know how to create an appropriate map for this new reality before we can start navigating the future successfully.

Multiple Personality Order

"The meeting of two personalities is like the contact of two chemical substances: if there is any reaction, both are transformed."

Carl Gustav Jung
Swiss Psychiatrist
Founder of Analytical Psychology

What are the implications of juggling three realities when it comes to one's personal and professional life? The three realities mentioned in the previous chapter serve well to build a collective understanding of where total connectivity will likely propel us in the future. But how important will it be to have a real grasp of the implications? Where will the anticipated socioeconomic and sociocultural shifts lead us?

You may have heard of a condition called Dissociative Identity Disorder (DID), better known as Multiple Personality Disorder (MPD). The *Cambridge Dictionary of Psychology* defines this condition as follows:

> *n. A disorder characterized by the presence of two or more distinct personalities or identities in the same person who recurrently exchange control of the person and who*

may have only some knowledge about each other and the
history of the person involved.[12]

To be diagnosed with Multiple Personality Disorder is nothing pleasant. However, as our world becomes more fragmented and complex, one could argue that a new condition is emerging, particularly among younger generations. We refer to it as *Multiple Personality Order*. While we are not categorizing it as a clinically severe mental condition, it is no doubt akin in nature to a Multiple Personality Disorder.

Symptoms of a *Multiple Personality Order* are an expression of the three realities previously discussed – *off the record, on the record* and an *amalgam reality*. For each existence, there is a different personality and quite often, one's *on the record* self is vastly dissimilar to one's *off the record* counterpart. Anyone born and living before the early 1970s essentially grew up in a one-way communications world. Expressing oneself required a deliberate act such as writing a real, physical postcard, let's say, or perhaps owning a camcorder much later in life to create something to get *on the record* for a little while. Other than famous actors, singers, politicians or any other public figure, no one lived *on the record* permanently.

The evolution, if not the revolution, of media through technological advancements has provided us with the luxury to be on air, *on the record*, published online whenever we wish. What once was a major undertaking involving expensive equipment and hoards of savvy media professionals, is now achieved through a click on Facebook Live. High-speed broadband combined with the very ease of appearing in a 'social newspaper,' (think of it as the Facebook newsfeed) has led to particular modes of behavior, attitudes and lifestyles. The idea of sharing one's choices and ways of living opens the gateway for creating new modes of existence.

We are not suggesting that millions of individuals have become popular celebrities. But it has suddenly turned millions of ordinary individuals into highly *médiatique* people who get more public exposure than any previous generation combined. Everyone can now leave a widely visible mark in history, or at least feel that they have. Essentially, self-expression and self-

---

12 Matsumoto, David. *The Cambridge Dictionary of Psychology*. Cambridge: Cambridge University Press, 2009

perception have spanned to an unprecedented extent, and the outcome is that status is no longer indicated merely through material wealth or by association with brands. It is also expressed through a public display of both verbal and visual information on individual experiences and feelings most often idealized towards the audience. The significance or insignificance of one's experiences and feelings is then determined by a thumbs-up or a thumbs-down. To be liked or not to be liked – that is the question.

It used to be that only famous public figures knew the feeling of being médiatique. Only brands and businesses with scale had pockets deep enough to buy media attention through advertisement, for example. Today, however, individual consumers are creating profiles in new channels and spending time, energy, and often capital, to develop them. At a certain stage, the profile starts to become a personality in and of itself, and eventually the online profile evolves as an additional personality. Perhaps the most prominent proxy to this idea is *Second Life*, a virtual world developed and owned by the San Francisco-based company Linden Lab. *Second Life* is similar to a massive multiplayer online role-playing game where users (also called residents) create virtual representations of themselves, called avatars, and are able to interact with places, objects, and other avatars. They can explore the world (known as the grid), meet other residents, socialize, participate in individual and group activities, build, create, shop, and trade virtual property and services with one another.[13]

An individual can organically make the transition into a dimension in which he or she might need to live out several personalities and know which one is appropriate in an online or a real-life situation. The implications of this state are related to maintaining a new kind of order – the *Multiple Personality Order*. From an individual's perspective, this order demands being well organized, maintained and managed. For anyone looking to 'sell,' it means understanding that the approach to targeting and communicating with audiences has become a lot more complex. Brands and businesses can now target profiles and 'personalities' to reach consumers on a much more granular level.

---

13 https://en.wikipedia.org/wiki/Second_Life

The Opinion Economy

*"It is one of the ironies of history
that people who live through a revolution
are least likely to understand it.
Nor do we realize where it comes from, where it is taking us,
and where the various currents within it find their roots."*

Dr Jacques Fabrice Vallee
Computer Scientist
Co-developer of ARPANET
(a precursor to the internet)

Aristotle concluded that pleasure is the only intrinsic good in life and therefore, it must be the ultimate Purpose to pursue. Life's aim was postulated as maximizing pleasure and minimizing pain. Because we derive pleasure from helping others, we can assume that if everyone maximizes pleasure, life would ultimately be good for everyone. Jeremy Bentham took this a step further with his 'Rule of Utility,' stating that "Good is whatever brings the greatest happiness to the greatest number of people." Advocating this on a collective level is what drives ethical behavior in our society.

The problem with this approach is subjectivity. Who decides what is best for all? Who decides what happiness is in the first place? If the power to decide over a question like this is left to one or a few individuals, then the outcome can potentially be disastrous. Human history has taught us a lesson or two bearing many examples of dictators and autocrats who chose what was good for them rather than what was good for the people. In terms of branding and marketing, this 'few to all' model is no longer relevant.

Figure 3: Collective Connectivity

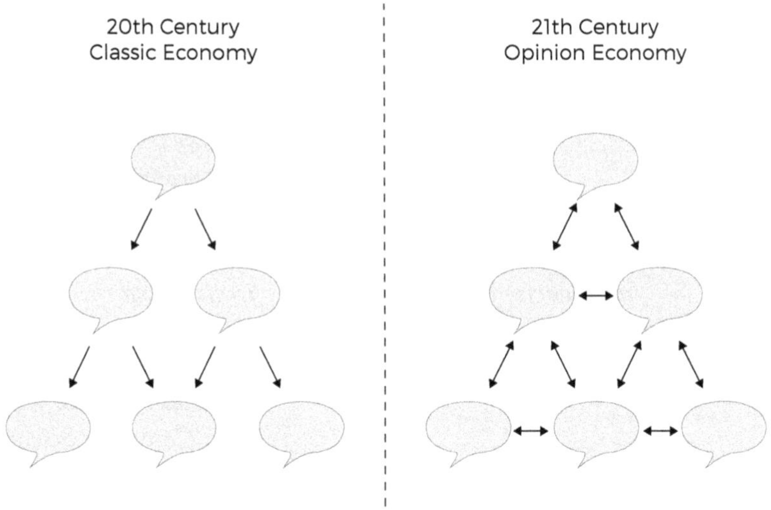

UNICEF estimates that an average of 353,000[14] babies are born each day. Apple sells about 74.5 million[15] iPhones in three months. That makes for about 827,000 iPhones each day – and Apple isn't alone. At about 20%[16] of the market, this translates to a ratio of about 11 smart phones on the grid for every baby being born. In the time it took you to read from the beginning of this chapter to this paragraph, about 100 babies were born – and over 1000 more people are now connected to the world of wireless communication.

---

14 "How Many Babies Are Born Each Day?" *The World Counts.*
<http://www.theworldcounts.com/stories/How-Many-Babies-Are-Born-Each-Day>.
15 Olson, Parmy. "Apple Smashes Forecasts, Selling 74.5 Million IPhones In Q1." *Forbes.* 28 Jan. 2015.
<http://www.forbes.com/sites/parmyolson/2015/01/27/apple-smashes-forecasts-selling-74-5-million-iphones-in-q1/>.
16 Statista https://www.statista.com/statistics/216459/global-market-share-of-apple-iphone/

Today consumers have unprecedented access to the technology that can make their voices heard. More and more individuals are joining the world's media ecosystem. Word of mouth, the oldest medium and certainly still effective by any means, is becoming the strongest again. It is *the* medium of today and tomorrow.

Consequently, the power has been placed into the hands of consumers – almost regardless of how much money a company invests in marketing. At the 2014 Global Marketing Conference in Sydney, Pernod Ricard's former CMO Martin Riley said: "Any ill-thought through commercial promotion in Thailand or Peru can come back and bite you in the UK or Australia. Today, brands are only as strong as their weakest link."[17] In other words, we have long moved from simple price checks on the go to a state of impacting the economy in much more fundamental ways, changing the very nature of how value is created – or destroyed.

The idea of *Multiple Personality Order* can make the alternative ego of a consumer inspire or perhaps conspire a movement against a certain brand or business. The potential is already there, and it would only take a few rebellious characters to trigger viral chaos. "Research shows that 90% of consumers would boycott a company if they learnt about any irresponsible business practices."[18] The 'project mayhem' that evolved out of *Fight Club*[19] would target a specific corporation by influencing the opinions of the corporations' clientele and staff. The film's main message is that the inner world of the protagonist was created to add Purpose to his meaningless life of sameness, boredom, routine and monotony. In reality, it is even easier for the connected consumer to develop a rebellious alternative ego in an ordered context than in a disordered one. In today's digital age, as Martine Riley warned, every brand can have its own "Tahrir Square or WikiLeaks moment." Eric Schmidt, (Google's CEO from 2001 to 2011) put it quite eloquently: "The Internet is the first thing that humanity has built that humanity doesn't understand, the largest experiment in anarchy that we have ever had."

---

17 Charles, Gemma, et al. "Brands Must Guard against 'Wikileak' Moment in Digital Age, Says Pernod Ricard CMO." *Campaign Brands Hub.* <http://www.campaignlive.co.uk/article/brands-guard-against-wikileak-moment-digital-age-says-pernod-ricard-cmo/1287257?src_site=marketingmagazine>.
18 Barton, Simon. "The Power of Purpose: How Purpose-Driven Strategy Creates More Value Than Growth *Articles | Strategy | Innovation Enterprise.* 01 Sept. 2016. <https://channels.theinnovationenterprise.com/articles/the-power-of-purpose-how-purpose-driven-strategy-creates-more-value-than-growth>.
19 *Fight Club* is a 1999 cult film based on the 1996 novel of the same name by Chuck Palahniuk and serves as metaphor representing a generational shift in how we consume, perceive and use media and the effects on our personality.

Entire value chains are changing. The commentary section on Amazon influences the purchase of books and much more. The opinions and ratings on Yelp or TripAdvisor have become one of the key determining factors when choosing a restaurant, cafe or a place to stay. The prettiest picture or the coolest brand video cannot repair the damage of negative ratings on these platforms. In times when a simple click or scan of a barcode is enough to compare pricing and service offers, the most fundamental marketing principles need to be called into question. However, the opinion of one individual has limited value. It's the aggregation of opinions that creates real power. Whatever you market, the only way to create and sustain value over time is to make sure you deliver integrity and value inside out.

Supply chain management was an offspring of the industrial revolution, a system to make processes more efficient. In our times, supply chain management is about value systems and transparency. Sourcemap, for instance, was one of the first platforms created for supply chain transparency across sectors ranging from pharmaceuticals to electronics. Leo Bonanni, CEO of Sourcemap, once claimed that "there are no remaining technical barriers to supply chain traceability."[20] As consumers we are no wiser than before. It's just that today it takes little or no effort to see if a promise of a better and cheaper product holds true. You don't need to have exclusive connections to the secret service to view the profile, prices or ratings of a particular brand, product or company. For the first time, businesses, brands and people are more likely to get caught in a lie or will be exposed for half-truths.

Marketing communications used to connect brands with consumers. Now consumers are connected to each other, so it doesn't really matter what you tell your customers on your website or on your commercials. Critical success factors such as positioning, differentiation, claiming a specific territory in the minds of customers will continue to preserve their key role in the discipline of brand building, but the means to achieve these have changed forever. Asking an advertising agency to do the makeup or polishing of a flawed proposition won't work. Brushing a bit of CSR (Corporate Social Responsibility) paint over an annual report of a company that delivers super low prices at the cost of exploiting people in another corner of the world is shortsighted.

---

20 Westenberg, Anthony. "Can We Unravel the Supply Chain?" *Thestar.com*. 29 Feb. 2016.
<https://www.thestar.com/business/2016/02/29/can-we-unravel-the-supply-chain.html>.

For people, brands and businesses, it is not just a matter of being honest. It is also about recognizing the changing context. Fish can't see water. The issue is that most of us fail to see the ongoing revolution of the opinion economy because we are so caught up in it. Connecting everyone with everybody (web), everybody with everything (IoT or Internet of Things) and everything with everything (Industry 4.0) marks only the beginning of what the opinion economy has in store. We believe that when value chains become totally transparent, the power will be decentralized and we will enter an era of *radical transparency*, making way for rapid, aggregated exchange of opinions – for better or worse.

The Viral Spiral

"Profit in business comes from repeat customers, customers that boast about your project or service, and that bring friends with them."

Dr W. Edwards Deming
Statistician and Management Consultant

When a brand is driven by its core Purpose, maintains its integrity and reaches the 'cult' stage for a group of consumers, it lends itself to an often-underrated medium called *word of mouth*. It sounds old-fashioned, but in essence, it is still the most organic and most powerful medium to opt for. At best, it neither looks like an advertisement, nor does it sound like one. Creative Director and Founder of Doyle Dane Bernbach (DDB), William Bernbach asserts that, "Word of mouth is the best medium of all." According to Nielsen's Global Trust in Advertising Report, 92% of the 28,000 internet respondents surveyed trust recommendations from friends and family above all other forms of advertising.[21]

If you grow your brand in a transparent and coherent way, protecting the trust built between your audience and your brand, early adopters can become the most influential advocates to communicate your brand Purpose.

---

21   Hall, Allan. "Take Charge of Your Brand Reputation Management." *CMSWire.com*. 16 Sept. 2016. <http://www.cmswire.com/customer-experience/take-charge-of-your-brand-reputation-management/>.

Harley-Davidson is perhaps the epitome of how powerful the effects of word of mouth can work over time. Emerging from near bankruptcy at the end of the seventies, to achieving cult status where fans tattoo the brand's logo on their bodies, required more than just a radiant brand-core. It took a management team that recognized how to build an entire world around the brand. They understood that building passion for the brand meant more than riding a motorcycle from point A to point B.

Consumers who belong to the group of early adopters voluntarily promote your brand's values and spread the word about your products and services with authentic passion. Joining the early adopters are the loyalists who may have made late purchases but nonetheless feel a strong bond as long as you stay loyal to your brand's overarching Purpose.

Loyalists, much like early adopters, become ambassadors and representatives of your brand, and most often even play the role of 'secret agents'. They begin to distribute positive intelligence, so to speak, about your brand, driven by an unspoken agreement. The beauty of this is that it never interrupts, disturbs or distracts attention. It's always within a contextual setting or mise-en-scène. In short, brand ambassadors deliver your message in the right place at the right time and often to the right people. We call this 'accessing the viral spiral.'

The most advanced stage of this craft of ambassadorship can be observed within the luxury goods sector. Whilst word of mouth is known and discussed in standard marketing, it hardly makes it to the priority list of today's marketing strategies. It's recognized as being powerful, but hard to achieve. It is much easier (and often faster) to spend marketing budgets on big campaigns to convince the masses.

Luxury brands, on the other hand, have been successfully running word-of-mouth strategies since the 17th century. In fact, it is still considered the best of mediums today simply because the product, or object of desire to put it more correctly, is always so perfect that it advertises itself. Indeed, the luxury industry does not see 'Marketing' as a discipline worth pursuing as such. Rather, it adheres to the so-called 'Anti Laws of Marketing,'[22] which we shall see later on provide interesting perspectives on how to win the hearts of audiences.

22 Kapferer, Jean-Noel and Bastien, Vincent (2009), *The Luxury Strategy*, London: Kogan Page, 2012.

In 1833 when Aleksander Pushkin, who is considered to be the founder of modern Russian literature, published his novel *Eugene Onegin* in verse, it was one of the most read works among the high society circles of St. Petersburg. In this iconic novel, Pushkin positions a luxury brand:

> *A dandy on the boulevards, [...] strolling at leisure until his Breguet, ever vigilant, reminds him it is midday.*

Luxury brands have never underestimated the power of word of mouth marketing. This particular product placement was made without a commercial agreement. It is important to emphasize that back then there was no such thing as the advertising or marketing industry. Pushkin simply shared the same fascination with luxury watchmaking as that of Russia's high society and featured a Breguet timepiece in what has become a classic work of Russian literature. Today, Breguet proudly uses this literary reference in their brand communications to great effect, associating the brand with poetic prestige. Genuine luxury brands cater to a small but lucrative niche market of expert customers. Like Harley-Davidson, these brands have masterfully created a brand-core that captivates people to such a degree that they willingly become influencers and advocates for the brand.

The advent of social media has brought us word of mouth on steroids. As we are on the verge of an opinion economy boom, this particular medium is now more relevant than ever. In this kind of economy, customers are influenced by brands only at a metalevel, and increasingly rely on 'peers' to make purchase decisions. Mass communication is no longer from few to all. It has become all to all. Not only do consumers get information about your firm from your website or from a close friend next door, but they also rely on the experiences and ratings of unknown consumers around the world. Who would have ever thought we'd trust the opinion of someone living halfway across the globe and whom we've never even met? This very dynamic implies that we have moved to the paradigm of the opinion economy in which the role of the players has changed. As Scott David Cook, co-founder of Intuit and a director of Procter & Gamble put it: "A brand is no longer what you tell consumers it is, it's what they tell each other it is."

Word of mouth functions as social proof and it triggers the viral spiral. It has to do with who recommends your brand or firm and gives it the legitimacy it needs to be underpinned with credibility. It's about getting positive references from those affiliated with relevant clients, partners, stakeholders, teams, consumer segments, etc. Word of mouth is still the only medium of direct interpersonal interaction, both on the record and off the record. It is important to remember that a word of mouth strategy is not only beneficial for B2C (Business to Consumer) marketing but also and in particular for B2B (Business to Business) marketing. In fact, analysis shows that business buyers are influenced by direct interactions with suppliers much more than anything else.[23]

Indeed, word of mouth is more influential today due to the rapid rise of social media and because company driven marketing is mostly limited to the initial stages in the purchase journey. Traditional marketing is by no means less important, but when it comes to purchasing decisions, the power of influence is truly unleashed through word of mouth. Through the rise of the opinion economy, consumers no longer decide on brands and products as linearly as they used to do.[24] It seems the closer we get to buy, the more we look to others to inform our final decision.

Startups generally don't have the same astronomical budgets as the global behemoths do. David Rusenko, the co-founder and CEO of the web hosting company Weebly said: "Word-of-mouth marketing is a crucial component of organic growth for startups and one of the primary ways that Weebly has grown to over 15 million customers." This medium is the engine that creates buzz, viral communication and endless referrals. But which brands have consistently been able to use the word of mouth medium throughout history? Generally speaking, it is the companies and entrepreneurs that define their core Purpose early on and then ruthlessly pursue it over time. A great proxy to look for input in this area is the luxury industry. Take Brunello Cucinelli's Purpose of 'humane capitalism,' for instance. His genuinely 'made in Italy' luxury fashion label not only pays employees up to 20% more than the industry average, but staff members do not have to punch time clocks, nor are they expected to answer after-hours emails – in

23 Cespedes, Frank V. and Bove, Tiffani "What Salespeople Need to Know About the New B2B Landscape." *HBR.org*. 02 Feb. 2016. <https://hbr.org/2015/08/what-salespeople-need-to-know-about-the-new-b2b-landscape?utm_source=Socialflow&utm_medium=Tweet&utm_campaign=Socialflow>.
24 Court, David, Elzinga, Dave, Mulder, Susie and Vetnik, Ole Jorgen. "The Consumer Decision Journey." *McKinsey & Company*. June 2009. <http://www.mckinsey.com/insights/marketing_sales/the_consumer_decision_journey>.

fact, it's not allowed. The company also donates 20% of its profits to a charitable cause.[25]

The Guiding Purpose Strategy creates clients who create clients. It doesn't buy an audience but builds audience that builds audience. A deeply connected, inner clarity for who you are and what you stand for is critical to accessing the viral spiral. The phenomenon of all-to-all communication is an indicator of the fact that the viral spiral is as great of an opportunity as it is a danger. To put it in the words of Dr Jef I. Richards: "While it may be true that the best advertising is word-of-mouth, never lose sight of the fact it also can be the worst advertising."

---

25 http://interbrand.com/best-brands/best-global-brands/2016/sector-overviews/the-luxury-reset-rethinking-the-growth-strategy/

Purpose Perspectives

Don't Hide Behind the Brand

"Unlike grownups, children have little need to deceive themselves."

Johann Wolfgang von Goethe
German Writer and Statesman

In embracing the zeitgeist, the new macro-context, it is easy to see complexity accelerating at a pace difficult to keep up with. If you or your organization is successful today, you need to be mindful of the fact that what got you here, won't get you there. However difficult it may seem, it is actually helpful to abandon conventional business thinking and detach from reality as we see it, even if it is for just a brief moment.

The luxury industry is definitely the place in which to look for brand power beyond the simple valuation of a brands' ability to capture people's attention (and wallets). Astute luxury brand managers are virtuosos when it comes to merging the intangible with the tangible to create desirability for their brands. Fueled with dreams and aspirations, these brands deliberately play with the risk of not serving certain clients. They often pick a positioning that is polarizing at the cost of excluding certain market segments. Luxury brands also play with pricing, often increasing prices over time. The one constant in the equation is brand. Because the brand is loaded with meaning and carries weight, it consistently earns the loyalty and trust of customers. A luxury brand is not just liked, it is respected for its name, a name that certifies and authorizes. A consumer is fully aware that many others value it as much as they do.

A common pitfall is to place either too much importance on the product or on the brand. It is a delicate balance that calls for mastery. It is actually quite a paradox that although luxury brands invest less capital in absolute terms on marketing than fast-moving consumer goods (FMCG) brands do, the value of brand plays a more critical role for luxury than for FMCG.

The reason why many mainstream brands fail to add value to their brand is based on an old idea that used to work but is practically irrelevant today. The idea that brand as an asset will do the work for the product. Or in other words: that investing in massive marketing campaigns is better than investing in the improvement of the product – which of course is a complete delusion. Although it is still observable in the non-luxury sector, there is really no need to investing astronomical sums on mass marketing. The product is one of the essential manifestations of the brand and when it is developed with meticulous care, it will create a pull. This does not just relate to quality, but to innovation as well. Think of Apple or Tesla. These companies have taught us that when you metamorphose and transform a product into an object of desire, it begins to sell itself, creating a rather nice dynamic of demand outstripping supply.

Not long ago transparency was just another fancy word used in business terminology. Investing millions in mass marketing does not necessarily mean investing in the brand as a whole. If anything, you are helping the marketing industry grow instead of helping your brand grow. Those days of hiding behind the brand are over. Producing weak products under the cover of a strong brand will not bode well with consumers – they can see you!

Today's consumers and those of the future will no longer trust corporate messaging in the way they used to. They turn elsewhere to learn the truth, searching instantly online to find out if a product has quality issues or if a company has been exposed for unethical behavior. You can shut down TV programs or censor print media, but online media is frequented by people acting as independent, investigative journalists armed with smartphones – and they are unstoppable in both speed and scale. The documentary *The Naked Brand,* demonstrates impressively how there are more videos uploaded on YouTube in a month than the major TV networks have broadcasted in the last 60 years combined.[26]

Supply chain management is being transformed on a fundamental level. Brands can no longer shift the blame onto other parts of the value chain. Connectivity and transparency have left companies and their brands no choice but to take full responsibility for their oil spills, child labor, mistreatment of animals and so on.

Total connectivity and radical transparency are changing the very nature of competition as well. Many of us still remember Toyota's failure to admit its faults. What started as a single, horrifying car accident in southern California, eventually turned into a global vehicle recall and the sales suspension of eight of Toyota's best-selling models, a move that cost the company and its dealers a whopping $54 million a day in lost sales revenue.[27] In addition to financial losses, the story that ensued was one of ignorance and denial. Toyota failed to take responsibility, which shook the solid foundation of trust the company had so painstakingly built up by producing good quality cars over many decades. Toyota as a brand was completely exposed, showing the world that it preferred to invest more time and capital on marketing than on safety.

Or think of Volkswagen, triggering one of the greatest scandals in automotive history by deliberately manipulating data. The engine software was manipulated to "detect when cars were being tested, changing the performance accordingly to improve (emissions) results."[28] Making customers believe they were buying an environmentally friendly car for the benefit of gaining competitive advantage was short-lived, as the company failed to take value-chain transparency into account. The German car company operated in a near dictatorial fashion, destroying its own solid reputation, losing one third of its market value in a matter of days. According to Burson Marsteller's research, 40% of a company's reputation is driven by Purpose.[29] When Purpose and the behavior of an organization are too far apart, reputation – the currency of our times – is shattered and profits decrease.

---

26 "The Naked Brand (2013)." *IMDB*. <http://www.imdb.com/title/tt2262281/>.
27 "A Chronology of How the World's Largest and Most Profitable Automaker Drove into a PR Disaster," <http://www.motortrend.com/news/toyota-recall-crisis/>
28 Hotten, Russell. "Volkswagen: The Scandal Explained." *BBC News*. 10 Dec. 2015. <http://www.bbc.com/news/business-34324772>.
29 "Purpose & Performance Audit and Diagnostic Tool." *Issuu*. 1 June 2010. <http://issuu.com/burson-marstseller-emea/docs/ppdiagnostictool?e=1598851%2F3341632>.

Some of our world's corporations are bigger than countries. Considering the fact that almost half of the world's top 100 largest economic entities are corporations, it is time for corporate leaders to acknowledge the reality that they have as much responsibility for the world's future as their non-corporate peers do.[30] It's time to start investing more time, energy and capital in brand value if you're serious about investing in the future. A bigger marketing budget will not necessarily lead to an increase in brand value. Real opportunity lies in mastering the ability to be a totally transparent brand that is aligned to a deeper Purpose. Repairing a negative image will become irrelevant as the new strategic approach focuses on preventing negative reputation in the first place. This is where the opportunity is long term. Brands that are aligned with their higher Purpose will stand the test of time, as they connect with their audiences and build trust from within. In keeping a solid consumer rapport, one becomes automatically attuned to the signs of the future.

---

30 White, Steven. "The Top 175 Global Economic Entities, 2011." *Steven White.* 11 Aug. 2012. <http://dstevenwhite.com/2012/08/11/the-top-175-global-economic-entities-2011/>.

Signs From the Future

"Any sufficiently advanced technology is equivalent to magic."

Sir Arthur C. Clarke
British Author, Futurologist
and Science Writer

Marketing in its current form is a dying discipline. It is being driven to extinction by a tech-savvy customer whose opinions are the new currency in a world of total transparency. Promotional effectiveness is becoming unaffordable, resulting in a spiral of increased expenditures to generate the same return. So where is marketing headed? What is the future of brand management? In order to answer these questions, we need to learn how to read the signs from the future.

Many of the devices we use today were depicted in sci-fi films such as *Star Wars*, *Minority Report*, *Star Trek*, *Avatar* and so forth. In 1865, Jules Verne wrote *From the Earth to the Moon*. What was total fiction back then turned out to be an indication of where the world was headed. Then he wrote *Twenty Thousand Leagues Under the Sea* in 1870, the source of inspiration for the inventor of the submarine. Verne then went on to envision the helicopter in *Nautilus*. Clearly, such fictional stories and their heroes have spurred creativity and inventiveness in the great minds of our times. Take Martin Cooper, the director of research and development at Motorola, for example. He credited the *Star Trek* communicator for the design of the first mobile phone in the early 1970s. "That was not fantasy to us," Cooper said, "that was an objective."[31]

Sir Arthur C. Clarke wrote about 'Geostationary Satellite Communications,' which basically meant online networks. Google glass reminds us of the *Terminator* who could immediately create a profile of the person he just met. Space travel, which has been the main subject of several sci-fi films, is becoming a branch of the tourism business today. Numerous other visionary authors, including H.G. Wells, Aldous Huxley and Isaac Asimov foresaw the inventions of our modern world. The astonishing and fascinating side of this continuing pattern is that these authors have the ability to illustrate such future advances of science in meticulous detail using the limited language of the times they live in. It is certainly a sound argument to say that stories authored by visionaries often pre-paint the future.

Karel Čapek, the Czech writer, was the first to introduce and popularize the frequently used international word *robot*. There is an abundance of films on robots that go beyond the man vs robot theme and address the emerging relationship between humanity and robotics or humanity and artificial intelligence (e.g. *Her, Ex Machina, Bicentennial Man, A.I. Artificial Intelligence,* etc.). These works communicate the signs of the future and how technological advancements could influence our lives, our behavior and our society.

We are witnessing the intensity and scale of scientific achievements in the field of robotics advancing at high speed. We already have self-operating vacuum cleaners, industrial factory robots, military robots, smart drones and so on. Boeing, Google and Boston Robotics are some of the leading brands pursuing the robotics industry in multiple directions.

According to futurists, some of the devices we've seen in the films of the last decade will likely become part of our daily reality in a shorter period of time than most people think. Moore's Law, for example, states that computer power doubles every 18 months. The key is to identify which authors are authorities in using their imagination. What's relevant for the new generation

---

31 Strauss, Mark. "Ten Inventions Inspired by Science Fiction." *Smithsonian.com.* 15 Mar. 2012.
<http://www.smithsonianmag.com/science-nature/ten-inventions-inspired-by-science-fiction-128080674/?no-ist>

of entrepreneurs are the subtleties that these futuristic authors sprinkle through their masterpieces. Their imagination is not limited to future inventions but rather encompasses the future of business and science. They give thought to how human relationships with science will change and with artistic license ask questions that are perhaps taboo among scientists, engineers and entrepreneurs. In the artistic space they can introduce the intangible that precedes the tangible. Marshall McLuhan, a Canadian communications analyst and futurist said: "It's always been the artist who perceives the alterations in man caused by a new medium, who recognizes that the future is the present and who uses his work to prepare the ground for it." We need the artists, the maestros and the creatives to help us set the foundation for the future of business, science and civilization in general.

There are several other sources of inspiration to draw from to spice up your company, your brand or even your self. Many strategists, managers and business leaders take these sources for granted. Lidewij Edelkoort, a Dutch futurist and design forecaster said: "Suddenly mythology and iconography are relevant sources of inspiration and at the core is this study of contemporary archetypes, drawing upon muses and models and oracles to design a future of fashion with a gentle and elegant hand." We have been receiving signs from the future for thousands of years. The trick is staying alert and open to them. Budding app creators, fin-tech entrepreneurs and scientists working on the developments of quantum computing and nanotechnology must broaden their minds in order to recognize these.

The R&D world of today refuses to take the word 'impossible' seriously. For instance, the notion of time travel, specifically travelling to the future faster than others, was absolutely inconceivable. Now it can be explained through quantum science. According to the Pentagon, by 2045 people will communicate using neural activity alone.[32] This means that what we consider as magic today will become the norm of tomorrow. As Sir Arthur C. Clarke put it: "Any sufficiently advanced technology is equivalent to magic." There has been more change for humanity in the last 100 years than in the last one million years combined.

Failing to recognize the macro-shifts in the value systems may not be a problem

---

32 The world in 2045, according to the Pentagon, *World Economic Forum* 2017

for your organization in the next five years, but it will be a problem in the next two decades ahead of us. In specific sectors and countries, not recognizing Purpose or failing to make it a priority may very well put you out of business in the 2040s. The implications on strategy are huge, particularly for companies with long-term planning cycles such as UBS, BP etc., anticipating scenarios for the next 50 years on issues such as how to source energy, for instance.

The luxury industry is the only industry that has always belonged to the Purpose club. Technology, media and automotive industries will most likely join before the finance industry. Private sectors in mature economies have already begun taking steps in the right direction. Some of the emerging countries are also making their way to the club, although many still operate on basic transactional value for lack of choice and progress in certain industries. The Edelman *Goodpurpose* study found that "62% of consumers in Rapid Growth Economies (RGEs) purchase products with Purpose at least monthly."[33]

Applying Moore's Law loosely to the speed of change in organizations, Purpose-led transformation will enter our lives a lot quicker than we think. One can argue that this macro-shift will be equivalent to an industrial revolution in its intensity and scope.

---

33 "Here." *Salterbaxter / Sustainability, Purpose and Creative Communications.* <http://www.salterbaxter.com/>.

Reducing Pain and Maximizing Pleasure

"The good is whatever brings the greatest happiness
to the greatest number of people."

Jeremy Bentham
British Philosopher, Jurist and Social Reformer

Many Eastern and Western philosophers in ancient times dedicated their lives to works that dealt with the philosophy of happiness. Hedonism is a school of thought built on this philosophy. Having a meaningful life guided by an inner Purpose that serves both the individual and the society is one of the most effective ways to successfully achieve and maintain a hedonistic lifestyle. Purpose-led entrepreneurs are already running new startups based on a hedonist agenda of contributing to the wellbeing of society. Where will this Purpose-led transformation make an impact first?

There is no doubt that health will be a macro-theme in the future. Medical science will become more precise and treat patients according to their physiological structure instead of treating everyone in the same way. While science may be objective, human beings are not all the same. Some have stronger bodies, while others have phobias and fears. Tasso Inc., an American startup, is already well advanced in its development of a device called Hemolink, which draws blood samples in a needle-free way. Hemolink collects enough blood for a broad range of diagnostic applications and connects seamlessly to trusted laboratories. Similar to the way Google personalizes your search results, your medical procedures will also be personalized according to your physiological and psychological structure. These are examples of companies with Purpose-driving progress in the field of medical science for the benefit of all.

Forward-thinking hospitals have made the firm decision to design their interior in the same fashion as luxury hotels – elegant and equipped with an entire sensory-experiential atmosphere. Several studies demonstrate that the design inside clinical settings can have a positive impact on patient outcomes.[34] Behavioral economics can explain how a classy interior design can reduce pain to the extent that the patients will want to stay longer even after they are actually healed. The hospital world wisely continues to learn from the world of luxury.

Dr Viktor Frankl, Austrian psychiatrist, neurologist and a key figure in existential therapy, explained how finding meaning could heal. As a Holocaust survivor, his experiences in the concentration camp were proof that finding meaning even in the most brutal situations helps one say yes to life. Surviving and escaping from that camp was statistically impossible for him, but finding meaning and Purpose in life helped him hold on to the very small possibility of surviving. Later during his career he published a book called *Man's Search for Meaning* in which he describes his experiences and how he came to believe in Purpose-oriented therapy.

In later decades, as Nick Craig and Scott A. Snook wrote, "doctors have even found that people with Purpose in their lives are less prone to disease."[35] A study, conducted by researchers at Rush University Medical Center in Chicago found that "participants with high scores on the life Purpose test were 2.4 times less likely to develop Alzheimer's compared with those who had the lowest scores."[36] There is plenty of evidence on how being driven

---

34 Yamaguchi, Yuhgo. "Better Healing from Better Hospital Design." *Harvard Business Review*. 08 May 2017. <https://hbr.org/2015/10/better-healing-from-better-hospital-design>.

35 Craig, Nick, and Scott A. Snook. "From Purpose to Impact." *Harvard Business Review*. 18 Aug. 2014. <https://hbr.org/2014/05/from-purpose-to-impact>.

36 O'Callaghan, Tiffany. "Sense of Fulfillment Linked to Lower Alzheimer's Risk." *Time*. 01 Mar. 2010. <http://healthland.time.com/2010/03/01/sense-of-fulfillment-linked-to-lower-alzheimers-risk/>.

by a higher Purpose is not only good for psychological health but also for physical health. In 2015, the Mount Sinai Medical Center conducted a study that showed that a high sense of Purpose is associated with a 23% reduction in death from all causes and a 19% risk reduction of heart attacks, strokes, or the need for coronary artery bypass surgery. The research team reviewed 10 relevant studies with the data of more than 137,000 people to analyze the impact of sense of Purpose on death rates and risk of cardiovascular events. The meta-analysis also found that those with a low sense of Purpose are more likely to die or experience cardiovascular events.[37]

On a fundamental level, it will not be about technological progress in and of itself. More likely, it will all depend on the Purpose of the world's inventors in developing the next wave of technological means. The goal will be not only to heal patients, but also to prevent or eliminate diseases and viruses. The future of health will focus on achieving the physical health of individuals and improving the overall wellbeing of civilizations, simultaneously reducing pain and maximizing pleasure in the process. Taking into account the Fourth Industrial Revolution, Stewart Wallis from the New Economics Foundation aptly stated: "History tells us that a value shift is triggered by creation of a new story about how we want to live."

---

37 Mount Sinai Medical Center. "Have a sense of purpose in life? It may protect your heart." *ScienceDaily*, 6 March 2015. <www.sciencedaily.com/releases/2015/03/150306132538.htm>.

The Blue Genie Effect

"We have a lamp inside us.
The oil of that lamp is our breathing,
our steps, and our peaceful smile.
Our practice is to light up the lamp."

Thich Nhat Hanh
Zen Master

Personalized technology is the disrupting force of marketing. As it drives and empowers the consumer, it influences (purchase) behavior, channels of choice and budgets. It is therefore no surprise that the 'technology factor' within the overall marketing expenditure has soared over the past decade – with no end in sight.

An exponentially growing tendency in the world of commerce is to blend advanced media technologies with customer-centricity. Billions, of dollars are being invested in consumer behavior research including big data and analytics, in-depth studies of the unconscious (neuroscience, psychoanalysis, behavioral economics, etc.), psychographics and so on. All of which will have paramount implications for the future of marketing. The direction in which the *why* question within consumer research is headed is leading us to a peculiar stage in the brand–client relationship. The consumer has more choice than ever and the brand wants to know more than anything who the consumer is and what he or she really wants. More importantly, brands want to know why the consumer prefers their brand or product to their competitors. In many ways, it is about predicting what consumers want before they know they want it. It is also about offering them something better than anything they could ever wish for.

So then the future role of marketing is metaphorically similar to the role of the Blue Genie from the oriental folklore. All the Genie cares about is being your best friend and he is dying to figure out what it is he could do for you to make that happen. It is not that your wish is his command. No, customer-centricity is not just about serving, glorifying or loving the consumer. It's creating meaningful bonds by crafting a product or experience that exceeds expectations and generates advocacy, lasting impressions and loyalty.

Again, it is the luxury sector that offers us excellent insights into the inner workings of how to achieve great customer appreciation. Paradoxically, most luxury brands probably invest the least in Big Data analytics and yet, they are closer to understanding how to get customers to rub the lamp than any other sector. Banks, for instance, invest a ton in marketing compared to luxury brands, spreading ads in which they merely claim to be customer-centric although they are miles away from being a *Blue Genie*. A few years ago, NatWest (Royal Bank of Scotland) ran a huge multimillion-dollar advertising campaign across the UK under the promising name of 'helpful banking.' The ads literally claimed that, "We have listened to thousands of people" and "That's why we are now open on Saturdays." This was certainly attractive to people working during the week. Sadly, only 675 out of the 1552 NatWest branches across the country actually opened on Saturdays.[38] In other words, two-thirds of the bank's clientele were excited about the offer and potentially visited a branch on Saturday only to learn the hard way that the campaign was a disappointing half-truth. Naturally, the NatWest brand suffered a loss of trust. As long as banks and other sectors continue to look at brand management as a pure enabler of more short-term sales, they will never become a *Blue Genie*.

It is no wonder that the coming generation of consumers trusts luxury brands, boutique companies, but equally large tech companies such as Google, Amazon etc. more than they trust the establishment of large corporate brands.

---

38 http://www.campaignlive.co.uk/article/natwest-hit-asa-ban-customer-charter-ad/1046592

Google is the perfect example of a tech company that does everything it can to reach the most personalized level of organizing and presenting information to those who seek it. The first version of Google was literally the same for everyone. Today, every one of us has a personalized Google search algorithm of our own in addition to a global and local one. With each use, recommendations get better and more accurate. In Google's case, the *Blue Genie* effect occurs when the search engine pre-recognizes what you are searching for and provides top results fulfilling your wishes before you've made them.

Meta-personalization, humanization and rationalization are among the key macro-themes of the future. Understanding and adopting truly customer-centric approaches to value creation will result in better products, services, experiences and overall humanize touch points between brands and consumers, rubbing the lamp in order to finally embellish what is within. Being stuck inside the lamp for thousands of years gave the Genie a crick in the neck. The time has come to let him out.

Heroes, Giants, Gods

*"If I have seen further it is by standing
on the shoulders of giants."*

Sir Isaac Newton
Physicist and Mathematician

Many of the ancient belief systems of humankind were based on personifying the great forces of nature. These forces became heroes – giants, mythological gods, angels, demigods, etc. Humanity and society as we know it today went through great shifts such as the Enlightenment and the Industrial Revolution, perhaps due to our human need to personify.

Aspiring to have infinite wisdom, as the mythological gods had, was perhaps what motivated us to create the internet – a technological space that provides infinite information anytime and anywhere. We are not claiming that the father of the internet, Tim Berner-Lee was 'led by the gods,' but gaining immediate access to knowledge accumulated over thousands of years is one of those achievements that has given us a god-like ability. Indeed, the internet is said to have a lot in common with the human brain, for example. The human brain and man's desire to emulate it inspire much of today's research in cognitive computing. By no means are we gods, but the mythological heroes our ancestors imagined have served as a source of guidance in our attempts to extend human capabilities. Philosophers dreaming about immortality have encouraged us to find ways to extend our lives. Today, we live longer lives and witness more events and phenomena in one lifetime than any generation before us. Future generations will live twice as long as today's average lifespan and see even more throughout their lives. They will live to be much wiser, as they will be around long enough to recognize life's patterns.

Yet, our well of inspiration is not limited to ancient mythological gods. Modern generations create heroes, too: James Bond, Superman, Don Draper, the X-Men, Steve Jobs, Nikola Tesla, etc. But what makes some heroes more influential than others? Why do certain brands invest in them so much? What kind of heroes should a brand associate itself with?

Let us contemplate three types of heroes:

Type 1: Fictional heroes with superhuman qualities (e.g., Superman)
Type 2: Semi-fictional heroes inspired by real world individuals
  (e.g., James Bond, Don Draper)
Type 3: Heroes in our society doing extraordinary things
  (e.g., Nikola Tesla, Leonardo da Vinci, etc.)

Consumers know that they can never be Type 1 heroes. Still, they can take on certain characteristics of one. Heroes and giants never fail; they are aspirational and have meaningful values that transcend society.

Engaging in multimillion-dollar deals with famous celebrities of mainstream culture as opposed to fictional heroes can be very risky. In fact, many luxury brands avoid working with celebrities in their brand management altogether. Aston Martin, for instance, refuses to hire anyone famous. A Type 2 hero like James Bond, however, is still a fictional character with fictitious human flaws and therefore, poses little to no risk. The key is figuring out which hero possesses those characteristics that best fit with your brand and can address your target audience without the risk of causing reputational damage.

The ancient Greeks anthropomorphized the great forces of nature. Zeus was depicted as bearded old man with a strong fit body. Poseidon, the god of drought, flood, sea and earthquakes was also portrayed as a human being along with many other deities. You may find it amusing that they believed in such gods, but if you look at modern brand communications strategies you will notice that we have the same inclination to personify things. But instead of attributing human qualities to the forces of nature, human beings now embody brands. As an instructive case study, let's take Dos Equis. It used to be an indistinct beer brand until it became the sixth largest imported beer sold in the USA.[39] When imported beer sales dropped 11%, Dos Equis sales rose more than 17%.[40] The turning point came about when *The Most Interesting Man* emerged. This bon vivant was the ultimate personification of the Dos Equis brand – a creation that ended up taking the product to another level. To be clear, this is not at all a success story of massive advertising. Rather, it is a result caused by the careful positioning of a Type 2 hero. It is a case of outthinking the competition, which is not the same as buying vast amounts of ad space to saturate the market. An even more nostalgic example is, of course, *The Marlboro Man*. While consumers may have a hard time identifying with tobacco wrapped in paper, they can easily sympathize with a masculine cowboy riding into the sunset.

What role do the heroes, giants and gods play for Purpose-oriented brands and individuals? There is a particular role that non-fictional giants and heroes (Type 3) play in brand management, organizational culture and entrepreneurship. Type 3 figures set the example and share their unconventional paths to success with the world. They are masters at setting new precedents. People don't do what their leaders say; they do what their leaders do. The 12th-century French philosopher Bernard of Chartres wrote that we [the Moderns] are like dwarves perched on the shoulders of giants [the Ancients], and thus we are able to see much more and much farther. This is not at all because of our acute sight or the stature of our bodies, but because we are carried high and elevated by the magnitude of the giants. In his letter to the English polymath Robert Hooke, Sir Isaac Newton wrote the famous words: "If I have seen further it is by standing on the shoulders of giants." The heroes and giants of yesterday guide the heroes and giants of today and tomorrow.

---

39 Schultz., E.J. "How This Man Made Dos Equis a Most Interesting Marketing Story." *Ad Age*. 05 Mar. 2012.
<http://adage.com/article/behind-the-work/story-dos-equis-interesting-man-world/233112/>.
40 Bhatnaturally. "Case Study Series: Dos Equis – a Triumph for Creative." *Bhatnaturally*. 26 May 2014.
 <http://www.bhatnaturally.com/dos-equis-campaign-case-study-a-triumph-for-creative/>.

In the case of luxury brands, the founder is most often the giant on whose shoulders later generations stand on. This is certainly true of Thierry Hermès, founder of Hermès; Louis-François Cartier, founder of Cartier; Peter Carl Fabergé who created Fabergé; Abraham-Louis Breguet the innovator of the Breguet tourbillon, Antoni Patek and Adrien Philippe who founded Patek Philippe and so on. These founders were not mythological gods but creators of worlds. One of HSBC's ads targeted at small businesses, entrepreneurs and startup founders takes an interesting angle: "Founders are just people who found something they love. It's never just business." The minds behind luxury brands have something in common: they leave traces and marks in history and in the memories of descendants. Founders are by no means superhuman; they are human beings like the rest of us. It's just that they have found their core Purpose in life.

Transformation of Value Chains

*"Lots of companies don't succeed over time.
What do they fundamentally do wrong?
They usually miss the future."*

Larry Page
CEO, Google

Dr Clotaire Rapaille, market researcher and anthropologist, who conducts research on the cultural unconscious, explained that after half a century of research he discovered something fundamentally different from all his previous archetypal findings. He found that Generation Y represents a global generation with a universal set of values, regardless of their culture, ethnicity or nationality. We can reason that this is partly due to the existence of a supreme network, a topic we shall address in the next chapter. The volume, the speed and the intensity of connectivity, enabled through fast bandwidth and low cost access points, is increasing drastically. As a consequence, we are witnessing the rise of platforms, increasing transparency and the elimination of the middlemen. Airbnb, Uber and others are prime examples of how the digital revolution creates a disruptive force and unleashes unforeseen challenges.

Generation Y needs to see and believe the brands' Know-Why. This generation serves as a proxy for what we believe is only the beginning of much more value-chain disruption to come. Post-millennial generations will innately look for Purpose-led brands. Their expectations represent a new era of competitive risks for traditionally geared companies. As transparency increases, consumers have the power to 'see through' brands as they look behind the creation of products for integrity and real, honest social responsibility. This means that brands will more than ever need to control not only their own operations, but also those of their entire supply chain. Consumers can and will eliminate corporations that don't behave well and back those exemplary organizations that demonstrate absolute integrity in everything they deliver. A Gallup survey on Purpose found that "when promise and behavior are in sync and customers are aligned with a brand promise, they give that brand twice as much share of wallet (47%) as customers who aren't aligned with that same brand (23%)."[41] Essentially, brands that fail to match what they say with what they do won't win.

Hermès, a French luxury brand, found its Purpose in 'Keeping Craftsmanship Alive.'[42] While Hermès is in many ways a true Purpose-driven brand, the company failed to control its supply chain, which eventually led to an unexpected crisis in 2015. All it took was a short clip posted on YouTube and going viral, showing the cruel slaughtering of crocodiles at a Texan animal farm used for the production of Hermès' handbags Actress and namesake Jane Birkin (as in 'Hermès Birkin Bag, going anywhere from a few thousand dollars to $100,000) demanded that Hermès remove her name from the Birkin bag with immediate effect.[43] This worsened the impact of the scandal and damaged brand perception and identity at a speed the company was hardly able to keep up with. Hermès began taking the necessary action to prevent such scandals in the future, but it paid a huge price for not extending its Purpose to its entire value chain. Clearly, articulating Purpose is not enough. Purpose needs to be lived internally and throughout the value chain in order to uphold the level of integrity today's consumers demand.

The tectonic shift towards digitalization and transparency are pushing consumers to look at corporate integrity. It is an indication that our beliefs and value systems are going through a metamorphosis. The consumers' opinion

41   Gallup, Inc. "A Company's Purpose Has to Be a Lot More Than Words." *Gallup.com*. 28 July 2015.
<http://www.gallup.com/businessjournal/184376/company-purpose-lot-words.aspx>.
42   Adams, Susan. "Inside Hermès: Luxury's Secret Empire." *Forbes*. 10 Sept. 2015.
<http://www.forbes.com/sites/susanadams/2014/08/20/inside-hermes-luxury-secret-empire/>.
43   https://www.cnbc.com/2015/07/29/jane-birkin-requests-hermes-to-remove-name-off-iconic-birkin-bag.html

is a powerful disruptive force to be reckoned with, changing the very idea of commercial competition. Technological paradigm shifts are reshaping the media, marketing and consumer electronics industries, but also the finance sector. In fact, cyber finance has become one of the most essential components of the entire economic system.

One of the earliest shifts in finance occurred when precious metals were replaced with promissory notes, eliminating the correlation between the value of currencies and the scarcity of gold. The age of digitalization has put the currency system through another transition, whereby no physical element is left to represent value. Everything is made of 1s and 0s. Only a small percentage of all the money in the world exists as physical cash or as gold. Such terms as online banking, e-finance, fin-tech, mobile banking and so on have become a daily part of our language. It is not incidental that Michael Lewis's book entitled *Flash Boys* remained number one on the *New York Times* bestsellers list for weeks. His book essentially examines how the speed of data creates competitive advantage in high-frequency trading. In addition to the speed of data, the role of crypto-currency is also becoming more important. Bitcoin is one of the early indicators of this. According to MarketWatch, a $1000 investment in Bitcoin in 2010 would be worth about $35 million today.[44] Bitcoin operates on Blockchain technology, a decentralized and distributed digital ledger that records and validates transactions across thousands of independent computers. The upside? Records in the shared ledger cannot be modified retroactively without the alteration of all subsequent blocks and the collusion of the network – essentially they are almost impossible to hack. In theory, this means we no longer need to put our trust into banks to authorize monetary transactions. Indeed, the fundamental proposition upon which banking is built is at stake.

But value chain disruption goes a lot further. Blockchain is an 'open source' or communal technology, for which no usage fees, royalties or other monetary compensation is due. Whilst a bank charges high fees for an international money transfer, let's say, Blockchain technology enables the same transfer at practically zero cost. In short, Blockchain has the potential to be a truly

---

44 "World Economic Forum. The Rise of Digital Currencies. Read" – *World Economic Forum.*
<https://www.facebook.com/worldeconomicforum/videos/10154516985311479/>.

powerful disruptive force: a network within the financial system can outweigh the functions of an individual bank simply for the fact that it can provide more secure and personalized services to clients at near-zero cost. But what makes Blockchain technology truly fascinating is that it is by far not limited to financial transactions. Anything involving a contract, be it buying a product in a grocery store, purchasing a car or a gardening tool from someone on eBay, the way we 'transact' today will fundamentally change forever without most of us even noticing.

Value chain transformation is without a doubt redefining business and the nature of competition. As Buckminster Fuller explained, there is almost nothing about a caterpillar that tells you it's going to be a butterfly. From our perspective, and taking into account the angles examined so far, we can only conclude that a collective movement is underway to return to an Economy of Qualities, where trust is no longer measured by what you say or promise, but by what you actually do, how you demonstrate it and how others judge you for it.

Case in Point: Airbnb
Embedding Purpose within a disruptive business model.

Airbnb is a company run and founded by a millennial generation who saw an opportunity in the simplicity of offering people a cheaper alternative to booking accommodation at hotels. A sound business idea that had a nice side effect: the fun of staying at someone else's place for an authentic cultural experience away from home.

Airbnb offers an interesting perspective to the extent that it recognized the power of Purpose and embedded it early on in its existence. A short analysis of Airbnb's brand video on the company's identity[45] reveals the essence of the company's inner Purpose: 'To Belong.' The idea of belonging implies becoming part of a specific community, which takes Airbinb's proposition way beyond the transactional ease of finding a place to stay at a lower cost. It now also stands for belonging when in a foreign place and culture.

---

45 "Airbnb introduces the Bélo: the story of a symbol of belonging." –
YouTube <https://www.youtube.com/watch?v=nMITXMrrVQU>

A Swiss traveling to Japan, for instance, can feel more like a local staying in a Kyoto residential apartment, even if it's just for a few days. The same is true for the other end of the value chain – people offering their places on Airbnb also 'belong' in the sense that they engage with guests and enrich their visit by offering insider tips. It goes without saying that 'to belong' also serves as an inner Purpose with which staff and wider stakeholders can identify.

We see more and more companies coming to the realization that properly embedding Purpose into the core of their business model is a necessity, especially startups and young companies. Some examples include Sourcemap, EveryMove and BetterDoctor. Many large-sized firms, on the other hand, are late in recognizing the indispensable nature of Purpose. It requires a certain mindset, willingness and the ability to see how influential and enabling Purpose can be. Tesla, for instance, has discovered its Purpose as well: 'Accelerating the transition to electric mobility.' The question is – is it possible to retrofit a Purpose to an organization? For young organizations with a brand culture in the making, this is a relatively straightforward exercise. It is much harder to integrate Purpose into established global corporations because Purpose sits at the very core of an organization's culture. Still it is not entirely impossible. There is an increasing number of companies global in nature and of considerable size that do run on Purpose; Apple, Google, Ernst & Young, HBR, to name a few. And the network is expanding.

The Supreme Network

"Learn how to see.
Realize that everything connects to everything else."

Leonardo da Vinci
Italian Polymath

Omni-integration *is* the future, although the concept is not at all new. Many key figures in the history of religion, art, metaphysics, Eastern and Western philosophy have contemplated it. For example, it has been a part of the dialogue among Zen Buddhists and Sufi philosophers as the idea of all being connected to all has something to do with the universal truth that the conscious *anthropos* keeps seeking. That which is alike attracts what is alike, and all is alike on our planet. Therefore, all is connected. The forests on our planet are like the hair on our heads. The rocks and stones are like our skulls and bones. The rivers are designed like our nerves and veins. The chaotic cities are like the neural circuitry in our brains.

One of the biggest advances of humanity was the invention of massive communication networks and the transformation from static websites to the Internet of Things and beyond. However, raising the quantity of connections doesn't proportionally raise the quality of connections. Where does the opportunity lie in a world where the speed, the quantity and intensity of connectivity keep expanding exponentially? Connection quality is what will determine real value in the future. New economies of quality will become part of a larger cultural shift towards an inner paradigm of authenticity, meaning and sincerity as an antidote to the twentieth century phenomenon of mass-producing more of the same. It isn't about how many connections one has, but rather how the quality of those connections interrelates. Similarly, it isn't about the number of brand associations that exist in the minds of consumers, but about the quality of those associations. Creating value, then, requires maximizing the quality (not quantity) of messages in order to build stronger bridges between brands and individuals.

If connectedness is already a big theme today, it is nothing compared to what's coming. Internet.org, a large-scale initiative led by Facebook, is bringing together technology leaders, nonprofits and local communities to provide internet access to those who are not yet connected. Virgin Group founder, Sir Richard Branson, shared a similar vision at a recent World Economic Forum: "We [Virgin Galactic] are planning to put up an array of satellites, nearly 1500 from day one and up to 3000 satellites over a span of time." Communities in need will be able to install small satellite dishes on the rooftops of homes, schools, and universities to get connected. Google has also launched an R&D project called *Loon for Everyone*. Its mission is to provide internet access with high-altitude balloons that sail through the stratosphere and create an aerial wireless network. Space X, founded by Elon Musk, raised $1 billion in funding to provide internet access to rural, remote and underserved regions around the globe. The plan calls for launching a constellation of 4000 small and inexpensive satellites that would beam high-speed internet signals to all parts of the globe, including its most remote regions. According to Musk, the effort "would be like rebuilding the internet in space."[46]

As of 2016, roughly 3.6 billion people, or about 46% of the world's population, have internet access.[47] There is little doubt that in the near future, even more people will be connected to even more people. More people will be connected to more information, and the Internet of Things (IoT) will begin to connect all things to other things. From the perspective of agriculture for

---

46 Kang, Cecilia, and Davenport, Christian "SpaceX Founder Files with Government to Provide Internet Service from Space." *The Washington Post*. 09 June 2015. <http://www.washingtonpost.com/business/economy/spacex-founder-files-with-government-to-provide-internet-service-from-space/2015/06/09/db8d8d02-0eb7-11e5-a0dc-2b6f404ff5cf_story.html>.
47 "Internet Users." Number of Internet Users (2016) – Internet Live Stats. <http://www.internetlivestats.com/internet-users/>.

instance, farmers will have access to better weather data, which can improve their profitability. Healthcare will benefit from new found possibilities in the form of closed-loop insulin delivery, activity trackers during cancer treatment, self-testing devices that will help patients stay within their therapeutic range and lower the risk of stroke or bleeding and so on. The opportunities IoT offers are quite literally endless and mark a new era in how we will live in the future.

But connectedness is progressively going beyond the 'net' and reaching deeper than a mere exchange of information. In a world that is gradually digitized, the value of physical connections will become a crucial antidote. The Aston Martin key is an illustrative example of the value of touch. To roar up a powerful V8 or V12 Aston Martin engine, you don't need a 'key'; you need what the company calls an Emotional Control Unit (ECU). Although Aston Martin has the technology and capacity to design a car with keyless ignition, the brand keeps it as an integral part of the customer experience. The key has been transformed into a symbol of prestige in a time when even your average Ford Fiesta offers keyless ignition. It is not an automatic connection, but a manual one, whereby turning the Emotional Control Unit connects you to something much larger than the car. As Friedrich Nietzsche writes in his book *Thus Spoke Zarathustra*: "All anew, all eternal, all enlinked, enlaced and enamored. Oh, then did ye LOVE the world." Nietzsche refers to a world in which all is not only interconnected, but it is also united in an ultimate supreme network.

Connectedness to such an extreme degree is perhaps difficult to grasp today, as the internet has almost become a biological organism in itself, a continually evolving brain, if you will. Artificial Intelligence (AI) is taking on thoughts through cognitive computing and Virtual Reality (VR) gradually replicates feelings and thus emotions. Skeptics already forewarn of the coming 'singularity' – i.e. a state in which technology functions as 'one' and will have the power to outsmart us humble human beings. But let's not get ahead of ourselves. Perhaps a better metaphor to help us apprehend the interconnectedness of the future is the neural networks of our brains. It is worth reminding ourselves that the Web is nothing (yet) compared to the network in our brains in terms of speed and complexity. When we use our brains to help us understand a difficult concept, we are actually doing what networks do, namely making associations, connecting, linking, contacting and so on. Metaphors are integral elements of human language, and human language works as a network-like system of codes, meanings, and symbols. The bottom line is that when we are unable to explain something complex, metaphors help us out. By association we connect a concept or a thought to something similar to simplify that concept and make it more comprehensible. In reaching higher levels of connectedness, the human understanding of universal truth will advance at an unprecedented speed. Our networks will begin to match those of our neural system where digital bonds between things, people and information networks will be like the air we breathe – invisible and essential.

Connecting everything also means cutting out the middle and giving rise to platforms that enable and facilitate exchange of economic value without the necessity to hold, store or ship tangible goods, for instance. Tom Goodwin, Senior VP of Strategy and Innovation at Havas Media, famously summarized the transformational nature of today's world, saying: "Uber, the world's largest taxi company, owns no vehicles. Facebook, the world's most popular media owner, creates no content. Alibaba, the most valuable retailer, has no inventory. And Airbnb, the world's largest accommodation provider, owns no real estate. Something interesting is happening."

It is important to understand that connections will not only intensify, but the volume and number of channels will continue to grow exponentially, too. There will be more information, but also new sources of information. Consequently, both large and small corporations must be conscious of the fact that increased connectivity and speed will not only make transparency more relevant than ever, but it will also intensify interdependence. Genuine transparency in business will become the macro-theme of future commerce. Already today, consumers can pull their phones out of their pockets and with a few taps compare not just prices and service quality, but also brand reputation. They can check if you are paying your employees enough or if your supply chain is sustainable. The fundamentals of trade have begun to move beyond monetary transaction.

In such an environment, the function of a *Guiding Purpose Strategy* is essential for brands and professionals who intend to stay ahead of the curve. As we enter this new epoch of omni-integration, the ability to find and clarify an overarching Purpose will be the key to success. Putting Purpose at the core of business strategy will connect employees, suppliers and customers in unprecedented ways..Purpose will constitute the tree of life, rather than industry expertise, and it will enable those who touch it to connect with an entire ecosystem of the organization – the supreme network.

In an opinion economy driven by a supreme network, building authenticity, honesty and integrity into your value chain is not only critical for success, but it is a question of survival. If these core values aren't integral components of your internal operations, consumers will 'see' this and switch to a brand that satisfies their modern demands. Consumers will simply tune you out. Their power to terminate previously untouchable corporations should not be underestimated.

Slow Death

"The greatest trick the devil ever pulled was convincing the world he didn't exist."

Verbal
from *The Usual Suspects*

Today century-old companies can disappear within a matter of months if they blatantly disrespect the trust consumers have put in them. Marginal price differences are becoming an insignificant aspect for customers when choosing one product over another, especially when the integrity of value systems is at stake. It is critical to recall that for the first time ever, an entire generation with common value denominators are emerging. The Purpose agenda will, in a sense, force a Darwinian lens over brands and businesses. The strongest and fittest will survive.

We claim that companies not implementing a *Guiding Purpose Strategy* will likely be facing a slow death. Perhaps this rather cruel frog experiment will help exemplify what we mean. If one puts a frog into heated water, the frog will jump out to survive. However, if the water is heated gradually, the frog dies a slow death. It isn't aware of the danger, so it doesn't bother to respond to the changing environment.

There are still many companies unaware that the world of commerce is in transition. We've already seen over 50% of the Fortune 500 companies disappearing since the year 2000[48] – suffering through a progression we call slow death. Mainly hit by 'digital disruption,' these are companies that also ignore the Purpose component and ultimately meet their demise, often to their surprise.

The 'too big to fail' expression has lost its meaning and relevance. Do you remember Enron, Panam, Blockbuster, Compaq and Eastern Airlines?[49] This is just to name few large corporations that were great at crafting long-winded and lofty mission statements, but failed to clearly define their core Purpose. These companies were once in the top five within their sectors.

Organizations that died like our frog weren't aware of what was happening to them. The greatest trick the grim reaper ever pulled was to convince global corporations that he doesn't exist. Death doesn't send you a Whatsapp or a Facebook message to tell you that your company – or indeed, your entire industry – has been chosen. It silently and perpetually sneaks up on you. The warning signs are scarce and hard to spot, but they are there if you are willing to face them. The most important question is often ignored simply because it is human nature to be in denial: is my brand or my company on the road to death?

If you take into account the democratization of knowledge today, you may realize that know-how is becoming insufficient. If you bear in mind that decentralization is at work both in business and global politics, you begin to grasp that simply owning the biggest market share isn't enough. There is plenty of evidence already that companies with a clear Purpose outperform those that lack it. J. Sheth, D. B. Wolfe and R. Sisodia explain how world-class companies profit from passion and Purpose. They demonstrate how Purpose led companies outperform the market by a 9:1 ratio over a ten-year period.[50]

---

48   World Economic Forum 2016, *Accenture:* <https://www.weforum.org/agenda/2016/01/digital-disruption-has-only-just-begun>

49   15 Most Memorable Companies That Vanished. *NBCNews.com.* 26 Jan. 2011. <http://www.nbcnews.com/id/41027460/ns/business-us_business/t/most-memorable-companies-vanished/#.VfCxc7QxE3E>.

50   Sisodia, Rajendra, Wolfe, David B., and Sheth, Jagdish N. *Firms of Endearment: The Pursuit of Purpose and Profit.* New Jersey Pearson Education, 2007.

In order to define strategy, the know-how is not enough anymore because today the know-how needs to be complemented with the know-where and the most vital of all: the Know-Why.

On Purpose

Essence and Appearance

*"Clients will always remember a negative experience
no matter how many positive moments have been shared."*

Andrea Soriani
Head of Marketing
Maserati North America

In Greek philosophy, the concept of 'essence' is of particular interest. Aristotle originated it and linked the notion of *essence* to the idea of *definition*, which is quite a useful vehicle for reaching pragmatic goals. In fact, the concept of 'real essence' has been at the center of much of the philosophical debate since the 17th century. Metaphysically – that which is beyond physics – to ask what the essence of something is, is akin to asking what that something really is, fundamentally, what it does and why it's here.

There is a certain kind of tension in any child's life as he or she grows and learns about the world. Much of this tension is directly or indirectly related to essence and appearance. As years go by and the child grows, certain events in life demonstrate how things are not always what they appear to be. Likewise, the essence of an appearance may be good. This tension between appearance and essence plays a delicate role in business as well. From our perspective, whether it is associated with an entrepreneur, an organization, a brand or even an individual, essence should not be confused with identity or soul. Essence defines the inner self, while identity is the appearance. Without essence, identity can be unstable, fragile, unreliable, uncertain and fleeting. We are not suggesting that identity or appearance is less important. Rather, we want to stress the fact that the function of 'essence' cannot be overemphasized.

Business literature on brand management strategies often discusses the notion of 'brand essence,' but there are still very few senior marketers who truly grasp the meaning of it. This is simply because most brand managers around the world are disproportionately focused on 'brand appearance' and give the crucial role of brand essence to little attention. Rumi, the 13th-century poet, jurist and Sufi mystic, said: "Either appear as you are or be as you appear." In the context of 21st-century brand management, we translate Rumi's great words to mean that it is time for companies to synchronize appearance with essence.

A survey conducted by the Co-operative Bank found that over a three-year period businesses that projected themselves as having a strong ethical orientation increased their market share by 30%.[51] Traditional ways of doing business allowed space for cheap tricks, but the days of shallow marketing are over. In other words, marketing is embarking on a new era in which outer appearance must be in sync with the real inner essence of the value proposition, the firm, or the individual.

So, how do we synchronize appearance with essence? First of all, it is necessary to keep the descriptive close to the prescriptive. In short, the worlds of 'what it should be' and 'what it is' must not exist too far from each other. The gap must be closed.

---

51 Bains, Gurnek. *Meaning Inc.: The Blueprint for Business Success in the 21st Century*. London: Profile, 2006.

Hidden P's of Marketing

*"There is something behind the throne
greater than the king himself."*

Sir William Pitt
1st Earl of Chatham and British Statesman

The famous 4 P's of marketing, as defined by marketing guru Philip Kotter, are no longer enough to define our market place. Product, Price, Place and Promotion are still essential in defining one's value proposition and answering questions such as how much to charge, where and how to sell and how to win customers. While these P's that help us define our marketing mix are still at work, they are also more than half a century old. They were very relevant helping brand builders and marketers navigate through the 20th century, but the world and its consumers have most definitely moved on.

Given our discussion so far, we believe the marketing mix should to be expanded by three additional P's: (P)hysical environment, (P)eople and (P) rocess. Physical environment, because we can no longer build propositions in isolation of their impact without considering the greater agenda of interdependencies. People, because we live in an era of radical transparency where opinions form a new currency. And finally Process, because value chain disruption is systemic.

More importantly, however, are the Hidden P's of Marketing: Passion, Perseverance and Purpose. These are perhaps the most essential P's, enriching the creation of a perfect marketing mix. Passion is needed to excite and rally people to create. Perseverance is seeing actions, plans and bold ideas through. And Purpose is what holds everything and everyone together. These three P's are often hard to spot because they reside in the inner world of an individual or an internal culture of an organization. They are less tangible than the creation of a new product, brand or marketing mix. Without these three hidden P's, all the others hardly have a chance of optimizing Return-On-Investment (ROI) in the long run.

There is a strong relationship between Purpose and Passion. A person who has found his or her Purpose can't help but show contagious enthusiasm and devotion to that which makes him or her happy. Not every passionate person has found Purpose, but those who have innately inject passion into whatever matters to them. As John Calvin Maxwell explains in his work on leadership: "People don't care how much you know until they know how much you care."

If college students came across more teachers and professors who were passionate about their fields, they may get curious about a particular field themselves and start to develop a passion for it. Understanding and mastering the hidden P's of marketing require us to be at least familiar with the language of Purpose and the contagiousness of passion. Otherwise, your chances of eloquently leveraging passion and perseverance will be slim. Remember the universal law of social interaction? Only boring people are bored and only interested people are interesting.

While Purpose with a capital P is not always readily visible to the naked eye, it manifests all around us. Research shows that Purpose-driven companies in the S&P 500 boast returns of 1025% over a 10-year period, compared to just 122% of the rest.[52] We tend to notice the extraordinary creations that stem from Purpose without giving it credit. Not all creation is shaped by one's Purpose and not all creation is meaningful. However, those creations that live long lifecycles withstanding the test of time are those brought to fruition by a deep, inner Reason-Why.

---

52 "To Go from "Good to Great, Be Endearing." *Good* for Profit. <http://causecapitalism.com/firms-of-endearment/>.

The Shaman and the Meaningful Brand

"The very meaninglessness of life forces man to create his own meaning."

Stanley Kubrick
American Film Director and Editor

When our ancestors first became conscious of their existence a new immortal need was born – the need to make meaning. Leading a meaningless life creates a demand for an agent, a leader who could make meaning out of all things in daily life, including nature and humanity itself. When conducting ethnographic fieldwork we had the opportunity to meet with Kara-ool Tulushevich Dopchun-ool, the Supreme Shaman of the Republic of Tuva, to discuss the inner-workings of Shamanism. The Siberians coined the term 'shaman.' Traditional Turkic Shamanism is one of the oldest, if not the first proxy to creating a belief system and spread knowledge in the pre-civilization and pre-religion era. The shaman was the one who presented value systems and gave meaningful explanations about the future, teaching that the source of it all was a deep Purpose hidden within each individual.

We've come a long way since the birth of consciousness, but our collective craving for meaning has not ceased. In fact, it has only increased. The relevance of an overarching Purpose in life is even stronger today because we understand that it is the source from which satisfaction is derived and entire cultures are built.

Our drive to find meaning and Purpose in life is what distinguishes us from animals. It's what got us out of the woods and onto the plains. The continuing evolution of man has sparked cultural progress, whereby a system of values has emerged. This changes everything. The more we evolve, the more we understand that it is a source of life, something we need to breathe.

In his book called *The Ad Man and the Shaman*[53], Ahmet Gungoren, a Turkish copywriter and cultural anthropologist, highlights the persistent presence of the human desire to give meaning. In prehistoric times, new belief systems and storytellers gained importance due to an urge to make sense of their surrounding world. The scientific revolution, for example, was the result of a deep human need to make sense of nature.

Coming back to business, we believe that there will be less and less room for meaningless brands, firms, products and services simply because it is in our human nature to seek meaning. If an enterprise lacks Purpose and fails to contribute to society in a meaningful way, its relevance will be put into question.

While there are plenty of marketing gurus, there are too few marketing shamans. But we can learn to be agents of meaning by comprehending that value comes from Purpose and that sustainable profitability is not achievable without it. The Shamanic question is: Are you and your organization ready to make the necessary paradigmatic shift and give your business true, inner meaning?

---

53 Güngören, Ahmet. "Reklamcı Ve Şaman." *Kitapyurdu.com*, <www.kitapyurdu.com/kitap/reklamci-ve-saman/24225.html.>

The Guiding Purpose

*"If we understood our cognitive limitations in the same way
that we understand our physical limitations …
we could design a better world."*

Dan Ariely
Professor of Behavioral Economics
Duke University

According to Peter Pearson, a marital and couples psychologist, the Holy Grail of relationships is about finding a person who shares the same core values. As time goes by, chemical or physical attraction can fade, but shared values remain a solid common ground. One can negotiate one's interests, but deep values and, even more so, one's guiding Purpose is non-negotiable. Spending your life with those that share the same core values helps you live a fulfilling life.[54]

Bronnie Ware, an Australian nurse who spent several years working in palliative care, caring for patients in the last 12 weeks of their lives, recorded the regrets of the dying.[55] She asked her terminally ill patients if they had any regrets and if they could go back in time, what they would do differently. The number

---

54 Baer, Drake. "A Couples Therapist Reveals the Most Important Quality to Look for in a Partner." *Business Insider.* 03 Mar. 2016. <http://www.businessinsider.com/the-most-important-quality-to-look-for-a-partner-2016-3>.
55 Steiner, Susie. "Top Five Regrets of the Dying." *Guardian.* 01 Feb. 2012.
<http://www.theguardian.com/lifeandstyle/2012/feb/01/top-five-regrets-of-the-dying>.

one regret was not having the courage to live a life true to oneself. Realizing too late that you haven't followed your inner Purpose makes you feel that you've made an irreversible mistake. The same goes for brands and businesses, of course.

Many people in their eighties today are not able to look back at their lives and articulate a particular Purpose. They may have had unconscious ambitions and desires that drove them to achieving certain things, but they grew up in different times where life was about survival for most people. Not only did they not have the luxury to invest time and effort in reflecting on Purpose, but it was also not perceived as something vital to life.

Looking back at the first half of the 20th century, it becomes clear that it is easier today for young generations to live a life with an inner Purpose. According to a Gallup survey, 87% of today's teens think that their lives have an overall Purpose.[56] For some of the older generations, living life with an inner Purpose was not necessarily sociably accepted. Often your choices in life were perceived as radical or rebellious if they did not fit within the social norms. Luckily times have changed. Now there is more choice than ever: women's rights and individual human rights have progressed, nations are less isolated, science, speech and commerce have more freedom, knowledge and education can be developed and explored. The reasons to find Purpose in life are perhaps the same as they have always been, but we now have more liberty to pursue this quest. Today's challenge is more about weeding through the clutter of choice and information to find inner meaning. While it is more socially acceptable to embark on a search for life Purpose, one must have the skills to pinpoint the needle in a haystack.

The same goes for companies and brands, too. When demand is driven by the economic value of making things faster and cheaper, a non-monetary reflection on values and Purpose seems senseless. The mantra has been to minimize cost and maximize (monetary) profit, so why bother connecting it to a larger, deeper, higher Purpose? The *why* question is missing in this very industrial mode of thinking. This is no surprise – it is hard to pause and gain consciousness of 'existence.'

---

56   Gallup, Inc. "How Many Teens See Purpose for Life?" *Gallup.com*. 06 Apr. 2004.
<http://www.gallup.com/poll/11215/how-many-teens-see-purpose-life.aspx>.

As markets become even more competitive and cluttered, companies begin to recognize that clever market positioning alone will no longer be enough. They needed to answer the *Why* question. Hence our view that Purpose will define the 'post-positioning' era. Boardroom discussions on Purpose finally ensue within those companies advanced enough to acknowledge the positive impact a well-articulated and embedded Purpose can have.

Being the first industry to acknowledge the critical role of Purpose, the luxury industry withstood economic booms and crisis, macro-shifts, industrial revolutions and world wars. More recently, during the financial crisis and after the fall of Lehman Brothers in 2008, the luxury industry demonstrated its resilience once more, outperforming most other industries and even recovering much faster and stronger than any other industry.[57] According to a report by Bain & Company, the global personal luxury goods market held steady amid geopolitical uncertainty.[58] The luxury sector always understood that in order to build a market that is truly connected with the customer, company leaders needed to identify and articulate a shared territory of Purpose that encompassed their organizations internally and externally. If we look at long-standing successful luxury brands, it becomes blatantly clear that Purpose is the secret ingredient in the elixir that makes the brand permanently unique, independent and valuable beyond the rationality of money and time.

57   Ro, Sam. "How The Global Wealthy Are Doing Better Than Everyone Else In One Chart." *Business Insider.* 05 Apr. 2014. <http://www.businessinsider.com/global-luxury-index-stock-returns-2014-4>.
58   "The Global Personal Luxury Goods Market Holds Steady At €249 Billion Amid Geopolitical Uncertainty." *Www.bain.com.* <http://www.bain.com/about/press/press-releases/the_global_personal_luxury_goods_market_holds_steady_at_249_billion_amid_geopolitical_uncertainty.aspx>.

How Luxury Brands Apply Purpose

*"In the real world of work,
Purpose finding is what leaders do."*

Prof. Robert E. Quinn
Professor Emeritus of Management and Organizations
University of Michigan's Ross School of Business

Against the backdrop of an ever more connected and empowered consumer, leaders, brands, products and messages serve as anchor points for entire belief systems. Therefore, demonstrating integrity in any form of business is no longer just an option, but a mandatory key to survival and success. Luxury brands are at the forefront of branding, fueling dreams and aspirations while simultaneously building loyalty and generating above average profit margins. Even during the financial crisis, luxury brands were growing at 10–15% annually.[59] How do they do it? What can we learn from this prosperous sector? In which ways do luxury business models differ from conventional ones?

---

59 "Communication Director." *Communicating Luxury, Communicating Leadership | Communication Director.*
<http://www.communication-director.com/issues/communicating-luxury-communicating-leadership#.Vg0WoROqqko>.

As Rebecca Robins, Managing Director of Interbrand, wrote: "Over the past 15 years of the Best Global Brands list, the brand value amassed by luxury businesses has grown from $25.8 billion in 2000 to $143.7 billion in 2015. For well over a decade, luxury brands have ascended. They were hailed as haloed protectorates of double-digit growth. [...] When the economic crisis hit, luxury brands were the most resilient in weathering the storm."[60] We analyzed the common characteristics that helped luxury brands maintain stable growth and we discovered that they all have one thing in common: the ability to be loyal to a higher Purpose rather than merely chase short-term returns. Regardless of the economic climate, luxury brands have stayed loyal to who they really are; and more importantly, *why* they are. The luxury industry not only creates the finest objects and experiences, but its companies are also excellent at managing their core brand equity, or in other words, their internal 'Know-Why.' Luxury brands adopt a holistic mindset, always aware of the fact that Purpose must be integrated across all business functions. This is, unquestionably, the common denominator.

Not surprisingly, there is a growing tendency for non-luxury companies to recruit executives and directors from the luxury industry. Non-luxury organizations are interested in finding out how luxury brands build and maintain desirability and prosperity by sticking to a clearly defined Purpose. Tesla hired Burberry executive Ganesh Srivats as vice president of North American sales. Yves Saint Laurent's former CEO, Paul Deneve, went to Apple. Apple also hired Tag Heuer's Patrick Pruniaux and former Burberry CEO, Angela Ahrendts. A pattern is emerging to gather strategic intelligence from luxury brand experts.

One of the factors that help luxury brands stay on Purpose is upholding family values. As many luxury brands are family businesses, long-term thinking is the normal mode of operandi. Not being subject to external forces such as short-term pressure and stock market returns, a typical business plan cycles that go well beyond a five- to ten-year term. Count Anton-Wolfgang von Faber Castell claims, "Well-run family companies are distinguished by sustainable values and human virtues." Quick fixes that satisfy immediate needs only and ignore the scope of the future are not an accepted way of operating for the luxury industry.

---

60 Robins, Rebecca. "The Luxury Reset: Rethinking the Growth Strategy." *Harper's Bazaar.* 05 Oct. 2016.
<http://www.harpersbazaar.co.uk/fashion/fashion-news/news/a38183/best-global-brands-luxury-sector-growth-strategy/>.

In order to understand how Purpose is applied among luxury brands, we suggest looking at the strong relationship between the famous Blue Ocean Strategy[61] and the luxury business model: conventional competitive markets are the red oceans, turning market dynamics into one big bloodbath. Being preoccupied with competitors paralyzes the vision of a company before it even enters the competition. The Blue Ocean Strategy, to put it very simply, is about aiming at either expanding the pie (the market) or finding a new pie altogether, rather than racing to get a slice of an existing one. So in many ways, it makes competition irrelevant. This is where Blue Ocean Strategy and the luxury business model intersect. Both look beyond competition from the get-go. If there is something comparable on the market, it is no longer luxury since real luxury is, by definition, a superlative good or service. Luxury is about elevation. Louis XIV, the Sun King, for instance, wore high heels. The French ruler was of very short stature, but every nobleman of that time regardless of height wore high heels. It was symbolic of their elevated status in society. Indeed, it is men who invented and wore high heels for many centuries before women adopted them, elevating their attractiveness in society. Elevation is about moving up in society, professionally, socially, economically and culturally.

Instead of aiming at creating a better product or service, entrepreneurs get passionate about designing or inventing something that is at its pinnacle. It isn't better; it is the best. But it doesn't stop there. Once they've created the best product, they create the universe around it and fill it with desirability. Gradually, this universe becomes a kind of 'small monopoly' that is so desirable that it is beyond the realm of competition. It is about creating an uncontested marketplace. Such a business model is based on being *bought from* rather than *selling to* – which liberates businesses and prevents them from falling into the unprofitable spiral of doing whatever the customer wants.

Luxury brands don't follow – they lead. Asking what consumers want is not part of Blue Ocean Strategy either. It's not about giving them what they want. As Henry Ford explained it nicely: "If I had asked people what they wanted, they would have said: faster horses." It is more strategic to give them something they've not yet imagined.

---

61 Kim, W. Chan, and Mauborgne, Renee. *Blue Ocean Strategy*, Harvard: Harvard Business Review, 2005.

For reference, we've constructed a handy index that can be used when faced with conundrums and dilemmas in the space of brand and marketing management.

Figure 4: Antidotes of Luxury Marketing

Conventional Marketing	Luxury Marketing
Volume	Value
Loud signaling	Low signaling
Foreground	Background
Content marketing	Brand journalism
Quantity	Quality
Overpromising	Understatement
Demographic segment	Psychographic segment
Mass marketing	Niche marketing
Popular influencers	Key influencers
Fast communication	Slow communication
Short-term mindset	Long-term mindset
Buying audience	Building audience
Mathematical progress	Geometrical progress
Expansionist growth	Vertical growth
Red Ocean Strategy	Blue Ocean Strategy
Comparative decisions	Superlative decisions

Continuous learning, transforming and refining know-how is an important factor that determines the timelessness of a brand. Luxury brands are brilliant at this. In their article on the scholastic nature of luxury, Andrew Shipilov and Frédéric Godart look at conglomerates LVMH, Kering and Richemont. They explain how participants of training programs usually don't realize that they are in a program. The best part about such training programs is that there is no one single authority that teaches. The protégé, the disciple, the trainee or the apprentice *is* the scholar, but also the wise one with valuable knowledge. The only teacher or mentor is the learner's inner dynamo that works through self-observation, introspection, self-examination, critical thinking, self-analysis and intrinsic integrity. The learner is forced to take the truth as the authority instead of taking the authority as the truth.

Many fashion brands manufacture their products in third world countries, primarily to save costs. Because they often chase volume over quality and integrity in what they offer, they run the risk of becoming a victim of controversy and scandal. Fashion products have short lifecycles and they respond to trends that come and go. Adopting the principles of timelessness would shift fashion brands into a Purpose-driven transformation process. Hard to do, but possible at the cost of reverse-engineering existing paradigms and structures, which would require more than a bold move to abandon short-term pressures.

Advertisements from finance companies often lack creativity and aesthetics in their messages. This is generally due to the fact that most finance companies make large investments in marketing but very little in branding. *Arithmocratic* thinking leaves no space for the aristocratic thinking. Working integrity inside out is key in an environment where consumer trust is at an all-time low. A change of value and belief systems and tapping into the transformational power of a brand could do wonders for the finance industry as a whole. Take the Swiss watch industry as an example. It leads the global watch market and is a macro-example of how the quantitative aspects of business such as mathematics, geometry and astronomy, can actually coexist with design, aesthetics and philosophical thinking. In the finance sector, rational thinking tends to dominate. Environments such as banking, asset management, private equity, hedge funds, etc. are driven by numbers, generally excluding qualitative analysis, subjective interpretation and behavioral economics. Consequently, the ability to create desire by connecting on a deeper, emotional level is often non-existent. In a time where Artificial Intelligence is on the fast track and algorithms have the potential to replace core-banking propositions, it would be wise for financial institutions to rethink their positioning and underpinning value systems.

Investing in the latest technology is not a solution in itself. Luxury brands are hardly dependent on technology, yet they still operate very successfully. In fact, they have proven that it makes more sense for companies, particularly tech startups to first keep up with changing value systems and base their propositions on these values before trying to keep up with the pace of fast technological shifts. Even having the latest technology in your organization will not help you withstand economic turbulence, nor will it transform your brand into something meaningful and timeless, especially if your brand still lacks an overarching Purpose. CRM (Customer Relationship Management) is becoming CMR (Customer Managed Relationships), meaning the customer decides when, what and how to communicate or to buy. CRM needs to be about adopting the right mindset and building an internal culture first, rather than just installing the right software. Startups and Tech companies can learn from luxury in other areas too. Take Tesla for instance, and its meticulous attention to both design and distribution. They are cleverly builing a vertical value chain, which costs a fortune (Tesla does not operate a 'franchise' system and 'owns' its distribution), but it gives them the competitive advantage of being able to control the entire customer experience very closely.

Other technology brands operating outside the conventional thinking methods of their sector include Apple and Nest (which was acquired by Google). What they all have in common is a strong sense of aesthetics, which they've applied to both product design and the business model. They have learned from luxury brands how to align Purpose throughout the whole organization.

What can fast-moving consumer goods (FMCG) marketing learn from luxury? Answering this question could be a book of its own, because FMCG marketing works in the complete opposite direction to the world of luxury. Veuve Clicquot revolutionized biodegradable, isothermal packaging as a demonstration of integrity and quality in their production processes. While the number of people consuming Veuve Clicquot champagne is dramatically smaller than the number of people buying smartphones, for instance, there are still so many FMCG companies that are not environmentally and sustainably active. As the name implies, FMCG is generally a game of volume, oversupply, discounts and thin margins, resulting in millions of wastage in a world that is in desperate need for environmental and ecological awareness as well as sustainable community development.

We would perhaps live in a better global society if advert messages were less disturbing, annoying, interrupting and distracting. Luxury brands are on the right track here as well. Luxury advertising tends to emphasize aesthetic values and spread messages with philosophical meaning rather than conveying a consumerist focus. A Patek Philippe ad provides for a perfect example of traditional family values: "You never actually own a Patek Philippe, you merely look after it for the next generation."

The Changing Nature of Consumers

"Some people think luxury is the opposite of poverty. It is not. It is the opposite of vulgarity."

Coco Chanel
French Fashion Designer and Businesswoman

Between the years 1850 and 1950, the world navigated through the age of industrialization. These times were based on a 'take to market' business model. Finding customers in an era where demand never ceased wasn't hard. Companies were primarily engineering-led and product-oriented, and the notion of truly understanding the customer was practically non-existent.

At some point in the late 1930s, Procter & Gamble recognized the need to differentiate and actively 'brand manage' products in order to optimize market orientation and financial returns, articulating the first notion of modern brand management. As competition started to pick up, the idea of 'positioning' emerged. Targeting and ideally occupying a specific place in the minds of consumers required an innate understanding of how consumers tick. Whilst somewhat more consumer-centric, this is still essentially a one-way approach to capturing markets (and customers). We call this the 'market to' era, taking us to about the year 2000.

Since then, businesses have started to recognize that putting the customer at the heart of their value propositions is the way to thrive in the future. This marks the beginning of the post-positioning era, moving past the 'take to market' and 'market to' approaches. Essentially, brands must step beyond the idea of understanding consumers (think about market research, focus groups, etc.) and embrace the concept of co-creating value with consumers. Developing a product, testing it, and then taking it to market no longer suffices. Value creation starts in unison with the customer.

Figure 5: From Product Centricity to Co-creation of Value with Customers

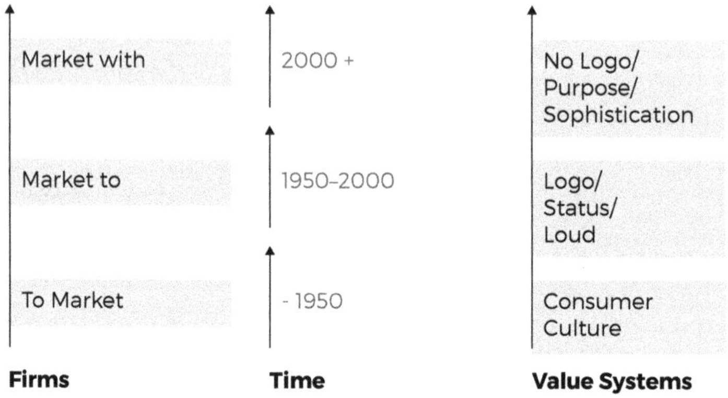

Firms	Time	Value Systems
Market with	2000 +	No Logo/ Purpose/ Sophistication
Market to	1950–2000	Logo/ Status/ Loud
To Market	- 1950	Consumer Culture

Case in Point: Harley-Davidson

Founded over a century ago in a shed in Milwaukee just north of Chicago, Harley-Davidson has emerged as a brand with the ability to withstand the test of time. Its power lies in the strength of its Purpose, one that has inspired generations past and present by offering a world of socially accepted rebellion based on values of freedom and independence. Like many companies of the era, Harley-Davidson was created by engineers who were passionate about the burgeoning possibilities technology offered.

Their first motorcycle was called the Silent Gray Fellow, a very reliable 'bicycle with an engine' that got you from A to B. Taking the Silent Gray Fellow 'to market' won the company a positive reputation: customer demand for the company's products picked up, especially during and after World War I when military demand for motorcycles further propelled the company's growth.

It wasn't until the late 1930s that Harley-Davidson realized the fundamental shift that would eventually change its course of business. Simply taking products to market was no longer good enough in a market where most Americans bought automobiles instead, or at least aspired to own one. Understanding what customers wanted early on, the company boldly repositioned its brand image as a lifestyle choice, rather than a means of transportation. The marketing approach shifted towards a purposeful 'to customers' focus, moving away from a rational 'to market' one. Movies like *Easy Rider* or even *Terminator* underpinned the rebellious nature of what the brand stood for and customers soon no longer bought Harley-Davidson for the function of the product itself, but instead for the experience the brand provided. Harley-Davidson managed to revise their story to one that allowed customers to break out of their daily routines and enjoy the freedom of the open road with like-minded peers – a message that resonated with the changing needs of customers.

In 2013, Harley-Davidson launched 'Project Rushmore,' a large-scale initiative embedding a customer value creation framework into their product development process by involving hundreds of riders from all over the world. Customer feedback was taken into the heart of the development process for the company's next generation of motorcycles. It's certainly not an easy feat for a century-old brand to stay relevant in the 21st century – and it doesn't happen by chance. It requires focus, dedication and the courage to see beyond the obvious to be able to successfully take a brand from the era of 'Build it and they will come'[62] to a place where 'Built by All of us, for All of us'[63] creates major appeal for customers.

---

62 Adapted quote from the 1989 movie *Field of Dreams*, symbolizing the nature of product oriented companies producing without taking the customer into the equation.
63 "Harley-Davidson Project Rushmore, Built by All of us, for All of Us" <https://www.youtube.com/watch?v=wR0hJ39YX0Q>

When exploring what drives change, it is often helpful to adopt an outside perspective. Looking at broader shifts on how customers, brands and their propositions evolve is what provides the strategic canvas. Luxury propositions are successful because they sit outside the rationale of value for money. They promise belongingness to an aspirational world, loaded with emotion, richness, depth and stability. Such brands can help us see beyond conventional wisdom, altering the way we think about marketing today. Full of heritage, history and legacy, luxury brands do not radically change. However, they do evolve and modernize to keep up with the times.

In the height of today's information overload, access to knowledge about luxury has never been broader. It comes as no surprise that many luxury brands have been quick enough to jump on the digital bandwagon, offering anything from Skype interviews with craftsmen to virtual 360° tours of their ateliers. Whilst digitalization is becoming more important for luxury brands, the growing attitude among luxury consumers is that offline is today's new luxury.

For generations born before the 1950s, Tesla or Apple may not fully fit the definition of true luxury. However, the complex but romantic relationship between luxury and technology is gradually strengthening for the post-Baby Boomer generations. Rolls Royce, for instance, organized a free exhibition in Saatchi & Saatchi London where visitors could interact with and experience the technological expression of their Spirit of Ecstasy.[64]

Among Millennials and the upcoming Generation Z, experientialism is already the new existentialism. Experientialist philosophy answers the top existentialist question raised by the great French existentialist philosopher Jean Paul Sartre who famously said: "Everything has been figured out except how to live."[65] In other words, status is changing; status is a transitional concept. What was once seen as a demonstration of power (think of Louis XIV and his status demonstration of social power, elevating himself by means of wearing high heels) has morphed into proof of status through the demonstration of wealth (as in 'let me show you my shiny, super-fast red car'), to status being a demonstration of taste and sophistication. As Coco Chanel famously said over 50 years ago: "Some people think luxury is the opposite of poverty. It is not, it is the opposite of vulgarity."

---

64 "Rolls Royce and the Spirit of Ecstasy" <https://www.youtube.com/watch?v=BSgtdjdyCn4>
65 <http://www.goodreads.com/quotes/6984-everything-has-been-figured-out-except-how-to-live>

In a sense then, being in the know is the new way of showing status. Let's explore the implications of this a bit more in depth.

Figure 6: From Existentialism To Experientialism[66]

From	To
buy	live
sharing economy	opinion economy
status	taste
communication	connection
own	experience
online moments	offline moments
show	**know**

In the US – which is the largest luxury market in the world – we can observe for the first time in history that affluent Americans of Generation X outnumber Baby Boomers, according to Ipsos' Affluent Survey.[67] So yes, it is fair to claim that as the luxury consumer changes, so does the concept of luxury – but it is not because of technology, digitalization or social media. Luxury goods are still mainly purchased offline. The underlying driver inherent in all recent generations is a craving for value – not in value of money, but value of meaning, or value(s) of doing the right thing. The evidence pointing to this can be found in geographies with a younger consumer demographic: 71% of consumers in India and 80% of consumers in China are prepared to pay a premium price for products with a Purpose.[68]

This dynamic becomes most evident when observing how new brands are being tested and tried by Millennials – and increasingly by the post-millennial consumers, too. When they try a new luxury brand, product, hotel or a fine-dining restaurant, one of the first things Generation Y and Z will look for is LEGS – Lifestyle Enrichment Goods and Services. For luxury (brands) it means going beyond function, beyond the aspirational brand worlds and beyond promises of status. In a nutshell, LEGS represents the customer's search for meaning. And it is being tested, 24/7 and without mercy.

66 Kramer, Markus, 2017, <http://markuskramer.net/changing-nature-luxury-customers/>
67 Ipsos Affluents Survey <http://www.ipsos-na.com/news-polls/pressrelease.aspx?id=6993>
68 Edelman Good Purpose Survey 2012

According to the Airbus Billionaire Study[69], those new to wealth are generally more impulsive, but over time they become more discerning. The desire for silent luxury has existed for years in European economies and we've started witnessing similar patterns in the Asian markets about five years ago. A well-known logo and a high price tag are no longer enough – discernment, sophistication and taste are the new norm. Indeed, this is the transition from Show to Know.

Customers are increasingly choosing brands based on inner meaning and holistic integrity, rather than look and feel or symbolic value. This trend is particularly apparent in China. A growing middle class, striving for equality and access to information is yielding a progressively sophisticated customer base. Russia and Middle Eastern markets are also traveling down this road, albeit at a slower pace.

Figure 7: The Evolution of Taste and the Implications on the Changing Nature of Luxury Clientele

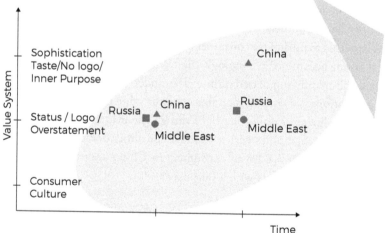

Time will tell how the next generation of luxury consumers in emerging economies will translate the idea of sophistication and taste. New research by Dr Stephen Kraus[70], SVP of Ipsos, also validates that today 'subtle and understated' are among the building blocks of affluent luxury customers' interest. Brands, companies and individuals with clarity of Purpose are changing the world for the better.

69 <http://www.airbus.com/presscentre/pressreleases/press-release-detail/detail/airbus-provides-insights-into-billionaire-buying-habits/>
70 <http://www.luxurydaily.com/wp-content/uploads/2015/04/07.Ipsos_.Steve-Kraus.pdf>

GPS
Guiding Purpose
Strategy

Decoding and Assembling Purpose

"The two most important days in our life
are the day you are born and the day you find out why."

Mark Twain
American Writer, Entrepreneur and Lecturer

In relation to businesses, value and meaning were once simple concepts contained in the practical aspects of a product. A formula was followed where functionality and utility would define a product, where the product was the brand and where the teams and people who delivered it were deeply connected with this modest but effective framework.

We live in times of tremendous change, macro-disruption and hyper-connectivity. As a consequence, we face a host of challenges and distractions that can result in misalignment, fragmentation, silos mentality, and in extreme cases, high-stress and dysfunctional environments. Let's not forget efficiency loss, which sadly often results in compromised productivity levels, if not low team spirit.

As the boundaries of our personal and professional lives merge ever more closely together, it is imperative that we look for inspiring and collectively aligned meaning in what we do, that we find our ultimate Purpose. But what is Purpose? How do we define and measure it – and most importantly, how can we find, articulate and embed Purpose within our organizations, brands or indeed within us?

According to the Big Innovation Centre, Britain's businesses could unlock up to $170b (GBP 130b) were they to set and pursue a clear corporate Purpose.[71] We are certain that this figure is just as relevant to many other economies as well. Differentiation, brand essence, positioning and raison d'être are often conflated. Actually they complement each other and should be seen as extensions, manifestations, functions or branches of the Purpose family. The innermost Purpose, with a capital P, is the divine force within a business.

If we analyze the very fundamentals of trade throughout history, we see that much of commerce has always been based on the process of transporting: importing and exporting products, services, intelligence, know-how, etc. In today's world, to be able to operate efficiently and profitably for the long-term, this list is no longer enough. We are living in an age wherein know-how must be complemented with know-where and most of all, with Know-Why.

The Know-Why of Purpose serves as the North Star, a guiding force that is constant and reliable in an ever-changing world. Following it will help you differentiate from competition. Once you accept that Purpose lies at the essence of a brand, defining a strategic brand vision, shaping the architecture of business capabilities and implementing organizational alignment will fall easily into place.

The Guiding Purpose Strategy Framework is the result of many years of first-hand experience of testing and adjusting methods and processes that help leading brands, their leaders and their teams find clarity and alignment from within. The *GPS Framework* is structured as a three-layered rose, analogical to the Tudor rose emblem. The central part of the rose is deep brand Purpose. The middle layer is composed of values, and the outer layer consists of more tangible elements such as vision, strategy, goals, etc. All elements interact in a continuum of forward motion, left to right.

---

71 Ray, Carolyn. "Aligning Brand, Purpose, and Culture – Views." *Interbrand.*
<http://interbrand.com/views/grow-on-purpose-aligning-brand-purpose-and-culture/>.

Figure 8: The Guiding Purpose Strategy Framework

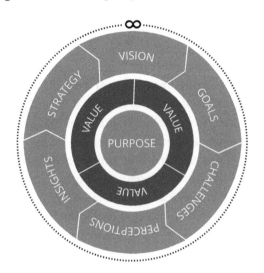

Most people are comfortable with expressing tangible methods of 'how they do' things. It is therefore easiest to begin from the outer layer and work clockwise, starting with 'Vision.' Most businesses will have a vision that generally reaches for the stars, which is a great starting point. Think of NASA's vision back in the 1960s of 'Putting a man on the moon.' It clearly states the ambition – but it does not say how to achieve it, let alone 'why' we should put a man on the moon. That comes later on.

'Goals' are more tangible and articulate what achieving success will mean. Make sure these are SMART (Specific, Measurable, Achievable, Realistic and Time bound). For example: 'Sell 50,000 cars by the end of the year.'

'Challenges' refers to the barriers and hurdles you have to overcome, including macro-constraints such as taxation, market access, strategic and operational issues such as cost, resource, building brand awareness, etc. For example: 'Low brand awareness' or 'Little internal resources available.'

Inside and outside 'Perceptions' are generally derived from active and passive market research, representing the voice of stakeholders (customers, employees, partners, etc.). For instance: 'The perception of price-points are 30% higher than actual.'

'Insights' distills Vision, Goals, Challenges and Perceptions into meaningful cornerstones to shape 'Strategy,' which formulates the 'How to' in succinct, clear and actionable language. For example: 'Focus on market entry in China.'

The second layer is where appropriate values are defined. This layer bridges the outer layer of 'how' to the inner-why, or Purpose. The best results are achieved by keeping the list of values to three to four important ones. Often two to three values describe a desired internal cultural behavior while one value clearly differentiates against competition. It is important to come up with values that are as unique as possible and select the ones that keep your company relevant in the future. Certain attributes such as 'Integrity' and 'Trust' are appealing to everyone and therefore, so commonly used that they are no longer unique and differentiating. Equally, if everything is a core value, then nothing is really a priority. We will address how to discover distinct values a bit later on.

Starting from the outside in as described above, the following chapters demonstrate the process of creating a cohesive, well thought through *Guiding Purpose Strategy*.

The GPS Framework

"Experience is the teacher of all things."

Julius Caesar
Roman Politician and General

Starting a meaningful journey of Purpose transformation requires first asking what business you are in: is your value proposition clearly defined? If you are Harley-Davidson, are you in the business of building motorcycles or fulfilling dreams of personal freedom? One question is rational and limiting, while the other one is limitless and hard to put a price tag on. Are you clear on what you sell, how you source it, for whom it is and how you sell it? How much it costs and what it returns? If the answer to these questions are either unclear or perhaps not clearly aligned internally, then it's a good idea to start creating a common understanding of the business you are in and how it works first, before moving on. Using a visual open source framework such as the *Business Model Canvas*[72] is a great tool to achieve this.

We assume however, that at this point your actual offering, or value proposition, is clear. Over time, we have been able to experience, test, experiment and synthesize what works best with brands, companies and individuals to guide them systematically from value proposition (business)

---

72 Credits go to Alex Osterwalder <https://strategyzer.com/canvas/business-model-canvas>

to articulating who they really are for better clarity. Simple circular rings indicate the layer of the *GPS Framework* you're currently working in. For ease of navigation, these can be found at the bottom right-hand corner on each of the following illustrations.

Figure 9: Strategy, Brand, Purpose

| Strategy | Brand | Purpose |

As discussed in the previous chapter, the outer ring of the *GPS Framework* helps us to put the business proposition into context. A linear description is helpful for this. The following diagram guides us in moving from Vision to desired Position. A ready-to-use template as well as examples are also available for download on the *GPS* website.

Figure 10: The Brand Strategy Map

Brand Strategy Map

Vision

Perceptions

Challenges

Strategy

Goals

Insights

TERRITORY OF OPPORTUNITY

www.guidingpurposestrategy.com

Moving inwards, we are now looking at the second layer of the *GPS Framework*. Whilst it is not our intent to deep-dive into the language of Brand Management, we will briefly touch on it here in order to help you build an understanding of how Brand Definition works.

Figure 11: The Brand Framework

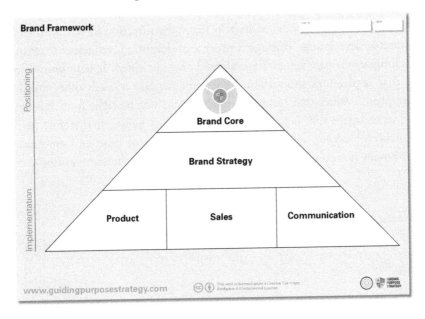

The Brand Core
Clearly marks the Brand Promise and positions the brand through differentiating core values.

Brand Strategy
Articulates how we 'deliver' the brand. The Brand Strategy is derived from the Brand Core and provides a 'how to' guide on consistent communications, which can be adjusted for respective channels and target groups.

Implementation (Product, Sales, Communication)
Internal and external audiences perceive the brand as 'relevant' and 'true.' The brand becomes the guiding instrument with which to shape and influence products and services, sales process and communication both internally and externally.

Our goal is to identify the values that best support the core. Values are used to describe a desired behavior and should be descriptive, unique and limited to no more than three to four. Each value can be articulated with words and images. Whilst it is easy to define internal values (think of 'trustworthy', 'authentic,' etc.), at least one value should be tied to differentiation and directly reflect the desired position of the brand. Brand Value definition should not be taken lightly. Through either existing research or tailored surveys, an initial 'Value Cloud' can be produced to help shape the direction in which to look for suitable descriptors. Through a process of definition, refinement, testing and elimination, core values are evaluated and identified. It is important to note that core values should also be complementary to each other and be future proof. Values that hold true today might not be right for a business or a market space that is undergoing tremendous change. It therefore helps to quickly plot your values against the dimension of time and emotional involvement (for consumer brands) and/or differentiation (competition).

Figure 12: Futuring Brand Values

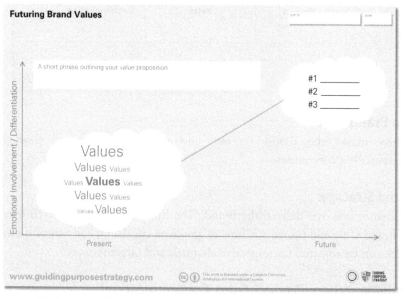

Brand Value articulation takes the final set of core values and renders these tangible. For clarity and context, each of the Brand Values is supported by a short description in words as well as a key visual that underpins the desired effect of intuitive meaning.

Figure 13: Brand Values

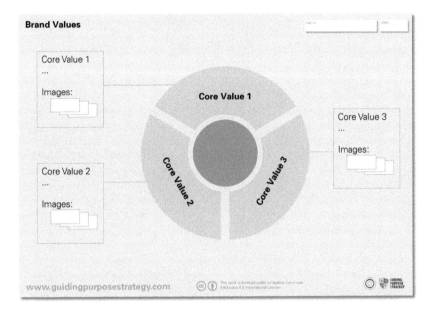

The appropriate articulation of Brand Values will build the backbone and architectural blueprint for creating the Brand Guidelines that will later bring your brand to life. This is not the subject of our book, but if you are interested in how this works please check the *GPS* website for further resources, ready-to-use frameworks, brand-value surveys, brand value books and tools to use in your work.

Seeking and Finding Purpose

"Logic will get you from A to B.
Imagination will take you everywhere."

Albert Einstein
German-born Theoretical Physicist

Because everyone has his or her own unique inner Purpose (consciously or not), it is best to explain the process of finding it by means of an example. Think about your fingerprints. The general pattern is fundamentally the same as that of the billions of other people. There is not a person on our planet that has a fingerprint that is different in its *overall* design. However, at the same time, every fingerprint is absolutely unique. Understanding this is key to understanding the framework for discovering Purpose. Like your fingerprint, Purpose marks your unique identity with the same universal system.

Having a clear idea as to where we are going with our value proposition, what the strategy is, how we want to position ourselves and how we want to articulate our brand, we are now at the very core of our journey. The *GPS Framework* laid out the overarching Purpose as the inner core of three circular layers. Getting to the roots of Purpose is visualized as the inside of a capital V – V for 'Voluntas,' Latin for 'of good Purpose.'

Figure 14: Seeking & Finding Purpose

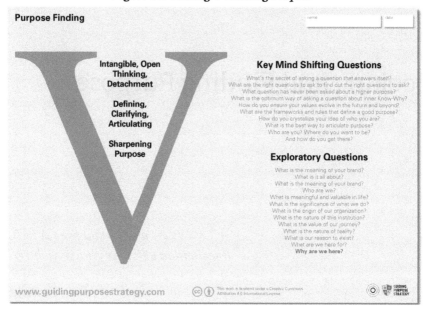

The top part of the V represents freethinking, openly exploring intangible notions, curiously wandering in detachment from the world of limits and gravity. The middle part represents defining, clarifying and articulating. The bottom of the letter V denotes the method of honing in on a singular, tangible Purpose. This process is systematic and holistic, moving from the intellectual to the practical. One must begin with the abstract and then venture downwards to the tangible. The process is driven by the need to adopt an outside-in perspective in order to be able to come up with a Purpose that radiates from the inside out.

It helps at this step to detach from the fast pace of everyday life and take an external viewpoint. This means escaping our daily routines to see the bigger picture. To be able to find our core Purpose, we must go against gravity and ascend high enough to gain a holistic view. This is difficult as there is a very powerful gravitational pull from the hot core of the earth – or in other words, our daily, operational tasks pull us back to the tangibility of milestones, deliverables and results. The laws of physics tell us that this force has the incredible energy to attract and pull everything to the center, keeping us in a constant gridlock. It is an undisputable *law*, but fortunately this is not a physical workout. Rather, this is a metaphysical exercise, so the laws are constituted in a different way. Whereas the pace of life will pull us generally back to rationality, this stage requires us to deliberately make time to detach. The direction is upwards, not forwards. It is an astral journey that broadens our thinking by dissolving conventional limits. *"Sic itur ad astra"* or "Thus one journeys to the stars" as the ancient Roman poet Virgil put it.

The mechanics for finding Purpose operates via systematic interactions. Reflecting on the following set of questions below will help stimulate the process of detached thinking.

Key Mind Shifting Questions

What's the secret of asking a question that answers itself?

What are the right questions to ask to find out the right questions to ask?

What question has never been asked about a higher Purpose?

What is the optimum way of asking a question about the inner Know-Why?

How do you ensure your values evolve in the future and beyond?

What are the frameworks and rules that define a good Purpose?

How do you crystallize your idea of who you are?

What is the best way to articulate Purpose?

Who are you? Where do you want to be?

And how do you get there?

Fundamental Exploratory Questions

What is the meaning of your brand?

What is it all about?

Who are we?

What is meaningful and valuable in life?

What is the significance of what we do?

What is the origin of our organization?

What is the nature of this institution?

What is the value of our journey?

What is the nature of reality?

What is our reason to exist?

What are we here for?

Why are we here?

Articulating and Clarifying Purpose

"The more original a discovery, the more obvious it seems afterwards."

Arthur Koestler, CBE
Hungarian–British Author and Journalist
Sonning Prize Laureate

What is the technique to articulating Purpose? How does one craft a good Purpose statement? Formulating such an important statement means finding the best way to communicate an organization's impact on the brand itself as well as the lives of its employees, customers, and surrounding community. We are now venturing down to the pointed edge of our letter V, where we start to solidify our Purpose by refining it with language.

This is the part where the skills of a wordsmith come into play. A careful choice of words steers us away from falling into the trap of short-lived clichés. Of course, all words with highly negative connotations; denotations, implications, associations and indications need to be eliminated right away. If you are not in the advertising, fashion, design or any other creative industry you might not be aware of extremely overused buzzwords. It is important to stay clear of these, so that you don't end up with a corny Purpose statement such as: "To make the world a better place." It is also important that you consider the subjectivity of your claim. What sounds intellectual to you may seem too abstract and vague for the people in your organization to grasp and make it actionable.

The entire operation of articulating and formulating Purpose is a very delicate process. We need the 'oenologist' to handpick every single word with meticulous care and with the utmost concentration. Word formulation must be more descriptive than prescriptive, stating who and why you are rather than what you do. If you are not being absolutely honest with yourself and if the element of intrinsic sincerity is absent, then you are missing the point. Apart from being clearly understood, your statement must be *instantly felt*.

A good Purpose statement must work intrinsically from within. It can therefore not be a lengthy, wordy expression that only you understand. It is also not a vision or multi-paragraph mission statement, but rather a combination of minimal words that maximize meaning. Putting your statement through a 'filter' can help you fine-tune its power.

A good Purpose statement …

- ideally starts with an action word (verb) that evokes a sense of movement
- provides deeper meaning for a brands ecosystem
- requires context that renders it universal yet unique
- expresses the overarching 'Reason Why' by relating to what you do
- is always true from within and a demonstration of utmost integrity
- connects with the head and the heart, speaking to both rational and emotional needs
- remains short, simple and memorable in ideally no more than five words

An issue that frequently arises when crafting Purpose statements is the confusion around 'Purpose' and 'Strapline.' Particularly for non-brand executives, the distinction is too subtle to be intuitive. Both are short and powerful. Both are engaging. Yet they serve for very different reasons. A strapline is often descriptive in nature at the inception of a brand and evolves over time to an elevated, intrinsic expression (i.e. think of Apple's 'Think

Different' or Harley-Davidson's 'Live Your Legend'[73]). A Strapline is catchy, often tied to a particular campaign and serves to differentiate for determined period of time.

A Purpose statement, on the other hand, is only truly intuitive and meaningful when understood in context, serving as the all-encompassing, philosophical canvas that provides long-term guidance and direction.

Case in Point: Apple

Steve Jobs had a vision: 'To make a contribution to the world by making tools for the mind that advance humankind.'[74] Apple does not operate according to a typical outside-in model, but rather adopts an inside-out approach, combining technology with aesthetics in new and innovative ways. With this approach, it inspires and attracts future talent who believe in making a difference for the sake of mankind, rather than simply churning out the next best gadget. Steve Jobs was obsessed with making things intuitive, safe and easy for us humble humans to use. Apple's overarching Purpose statement can aptly be summarized as 'Humanizing Technology' – two powerful words, loaded with meaning when understood in context. And with it, Steve Jobs proved to the world that the complexity of technology could coexist in harmony with aesthetic simplicity. Apple's ensuing breakthrough strapline 'Think Different' appealed to the creative minds, setting Apple apart from its PC rivals.

Apple's 2017 mission statement? Well, here it is:

'Apple designs Macs, the best personal computers in the world, along with OS X, iLife, iWork and professional software. Apple leads the digital music revolution with its iPods and iTunes online store. Apple has reinvented the mobile phone with its revolutionary iPhone and App store, and is defining the future of mobile media and computing devices with iPad.'

---

73 Stein, L. "Live Your Legend: Urges Harley-Davidson in New Global Campaign"
<http://adage.com/article/agency -news/harley-davidson-aims-energize-brand -campaign/303141/>
74 <http://www.investopedia.com/ask/answers/042315/what-apples-current-mission-statement-and-how-does-it-differ-steve-jobs-original-ideals.asp>

Clearly, Apple is a much larger company today than back in the days when a small team of geeks gave every bit of their energy to change the world. One can argue that mission statements change over time and that as companies grow, they become more 'hands on.' However, Purpose endures. Apple is still in the business of 'Humanizing Technology.'

As Steven Pinker, the cognitive scientist, states in his book *The Sense of Style*: "Governments and corporations have found that small improvements in clarity can prevent vast amounts of error, frustration, and waste…"[75] It isn't incidental that in our age of clutter the number one bestseller on Amazon (selling over two million copies) is a book about the Japanese art of de-cluttering and organizing.[76] The more clutter there is in our minds, the more difficult it is to clearly articulate a Purpose statement. In the end, it's about having the skills to condense and compress your deepest, most inner beliefs into universal meaningfulness.

Figure 15: Purpose Articulation

75 Pinker, Steven. *The Sense of Style the Thinking Person's Guide to Writing in the 21st Century*. London: Penguin, 2015.
76 Kondo, Marie. *Life-changing Magic: A Journal: Spark Joy Every Day*. Berkeley: Ten Speed, 2016.

If vision is where you are going, the brand an expression of who you are and strategy how you get there, then Purpose is *why* you do what you do. The *GPS Framework* helps translate the intrinsic nature of Purpose into something tangible that eventually evolves into a core Purpose statement. The aim is to maintain universal meaning easy enough to grasp. In the words of the French political writer Francois Gautier: "More important than the quest for certainty is the quest for clarity."

Shared and Aligned Purpose

"If two things are equal to the same thing,
they are equal to each other."

Euclid of Alexandria
Father of Geometry

A powerful and well-functioning Purpose aligns vertically as well as horizontally. In other words, it is shared and aligned within a brand's ecosystem.

Here is a good test for you to try. Take a minute and answer the following questions:

1. What is your Purpose? Can you articulate your answer in five words or less?

2. Now ask your peers, colleagues and boss: What is our Purpose? Can they articulate this in five words or less? If their answer is coherent with your answer to question 1, then you can claim 'shared Purpose.'

3. To gain an external perspective, ask your customers, suppliers and business partners: What do we stand for, what is our Purpose? If they give you the same answer as your internal colleagues, you can claim 'aligned Purpose.'

It is very rare for people to achieve cohesion on these three simple questions. Most people cannot even articulate an answer to the first question, let alone achieve coherence on questions 2 and 3.

If you answered all three questions with ease, this is the place to stop reading. Skip this chapter (or most of this book, in fact) and work on your strategy of 'how' to make things happen.

Figure 16: Shared & Aligned Purpose:

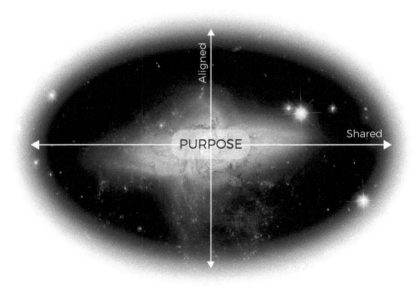

Creating shared and aligned Purpose is not as easy as the above test implies. It requires deep thinking and engagement on a cultural level. The process of 'soul-searching' to find Purpose is often triggered by a necessary market alignment, a repositioning, a need for change, rapid growth etc.

Research conducted by the American Management Association revealed that in organizations with more than 1000 employees, 61% of respondents considered staff to be less loyal now, compared to 2010.[77] Low morale was the most commonly identified consequence of decreasing loyalty (84%),

---

77 "Survey Finds Employees Less Loyal Than Five Years Ago." 01 June 2015. <http://www.amanet.org/news/10606.aspx>.

followed by high turnover and disengagement (80%), growing distrust amongst colleagues (76%), and lack of team spirit (73%).[78]

These are disturbing figures. Yet, when we ask directors, managers and executives, "What is your company's most valuable asset?" they reply with a cliché: "Our people." However, this is sadly flawed because firstly people are not 'assets' and secondly, people come and go. Your brand is the only thing that stays. It embodies every aspect of your company, including your people. Earlier we discussed the power of brand and that if managed carefully and consistently, it can create tremendous value over time.

Professor Chris Roebuck, a British economist who advises top organizations on maximizing performance through effective leadership, asked Aston Martin's CMO at the time about the company's Customer Relationship Management (CRM) system in order to better understand the link between CRM and effective leadership. The answer was as unexpected as it was candid, "We don't have one – yet it works." In other words, successful relationship management is not about the system, the infrastructure or technology only, it is first and foremost about the internal mindset that lies at the heart of an organizational culture. The catalyst of the mindset, the guiding compass and the path to an interconnected culture is rooted in the brand's inner Purpose. Technology can certainly add value in terms of empowering people with tools and information, but it can't replace the deeply ingrained Purpose that radiates from within. If shared and aligned internally and externally, Purpose has the power to unleash the type of passion, cohesion and consistency no CRM system has yet managed to replicate.

A Purpose-driven brand becomes the passing torch of enthusiasm and passion of *why* you do what you do. One of the key responsibilities of marketing leaders today then, other than making sure short-term targets are hit, is to facilitate and distribute the glue that builds and holds a brand together for the long-term.

---

78 "Employee Loyalty Is a Rare Commodity." *CGMA*. 13 Feb. 2015. |
<http://www.cgma.org/magazine/news/pages/201511807.aspx?TestCookiesEnabled=redirect>.

Case in Point: P1 Graphene Solutions

2D Technology is a Startup based in London and New York taking advantage of science and technology in the rapidly evolving world of wonder materials. Graphene makes things stronger; it's the most resistant and impermeable membrane ever. It's 200x stronger and 6x lighter than steel, extremely thin, transparent and bendable. It's also faster; electron mobility is 70x higher than in silicon and conducts heat 10x better than copper.

A key issue in this market is the sheer limitless opportunities the coming graphene revolution promises. Starting with the Business Model Canvas, the Startup decided to focus its efforts on translating the 'mad graphene science' into actionable traction for the motorsports and high-end car segment first, before branching out into other transport related fields – and consequently also 'adjusted' its still young name to P1 Graphene Solutions. Today, P1 Graphene is in the business of creating custom solutions for the application of graphene within the automotive sector. Specifically, this results in lower vehicle weight, less emissions and improved fuel efficiency.

Working through the outer ring of the *GPS Framework*, we first firm up the company's vision and its goals, identifying its territory of opportunity. From there we work through the challenges to overcome, we look at perceptions, derive insights and formulate a strategic direction leading to a desired future. P1 Graphene's bold vision is '*To take Graphene from Cars to Mars.*' A full example of P1 Graphene's Brand Strategy Map can be found in the resource section on the *GPS* website.

Moving one layer inside the *GPS Framework* requires us to think through P1 Graphene's value system. Which values will drive the desired behavior in the future, which ones can help differentiate the company in an industry that is mostly driven by scientists? Articulating the companies value system resulted in the following core values: *Pioneering, Collaborative and Focused.*

So then, what is P1 Graphene's raison d'être? We first come back to our Purpose statement checklist: keep it short and simple, ideally start with an action word, provide deeper meaning, make it contextual and make it true from within, – all ideally expressed in no more than five words.

This is the point where we need to detach from the tangible work we've done so far. This is also the moment where individual reflection is needed before the power of collective alignment can produce a suitable shared and aligned Purpose statement.

In practical terms, it helps to simply hand out post-it notes, pull up some of the mind-shifting and exploratory questions of the V-formula and ask people to reflect, think and articulate possible Purpose statements – individually, one per Post-it. Simply grouping the Purpose Post-its allows us to cluster the collective thinking. Sure, you will have to separate 'strapline' thinking from the deeper reflections pointing towards the inner Know-Why, but that's a relatively easy exercise. You can't expect a final product either, but it will get you about 80% there – no need for lengthy year-long thinking retreats and countless brainstorms causing more confusion than clarity. The remaining 20% of effort is about going through the Purpose statement checklist and articulating supporting context.

P1 Graphene's Purpose statement is: *Positively Transforming Performance.* Just three words sum up the positive impact on materials, people, processes and the output that ultimately benefits clients and the world at large. P1 Graphene's Purpose statement describes more than the way the company does things. It describes who they are and *why* they do what they do.

131

Measuring Purpose

"Measure what is measurable, and make measurable what is not so."

Galileo Galilei
Italian Mathematician and Physician

Something nonexistent starts to exist the moment we measure it. Today, quantum physicists can explain through mathematic measurements how something *is*. We've all had our first experiences with measuring starting back in elementary school. How could we ever forget our first ruler? The word 'ruler' also means the sovereign or the supreme authority that defines the rules to run an establishment, a tribe or a nation. We tend to forget that there is an intimate relationship between the capability to rule and the ability to measure.

It is helpful to bear in mind that identifying *what* is to be measured is as crucial as knowing how it will be measured. While the role of measuring is very important in the realm of business, it is often misunderstood. The luxury industry adopts an interesting to measuring 'success'. Unlike many other industries, luxury companies don't measure success by how many products they sell. And when it comes to brand communication strategies, success is not measured by how many consumers have seen an advertisement or read a promotional message.

The luxury industry considers the *who*, not the 'how many' as a significant indicator of success. Or in other words, measurement is based on quality, not quantity. Dr William Edwards Deming created the concept of Total Quality Management or TQM. It was this very concept that put postwar Japan on the map of the most powerful economies in the world. Despite being a statistician, Dr Deming believed that, "The most important things cannot be measured." With regards to long-term values, strategy and vision, quantity is almost always prioritized over quality in all sectors except the luxury sector. Case in point – *quam bene non quantum* (quality over quantity) is the motto we suggest for success in the 21st century.

Measuring Purpose within a company's culture requires establishing whether Purpose can maintain its position of relevance. If not, values need to be adjusted to match the inner Purpose. In order to test and verify if Purpose is still shared and aligned within your organization, leaders must cultivate an open dialogue with their employees, suppliers, customers and extended stakeholders.

Like consumer loyalty, employee loyalty needs to be built over time. Branding and social media specialist Simon Mainwaring says: "Ensure your employees understand what your brand stands for so they can be your first line of word-of-mouth advertising." Accessing the viral spiral applies not only to B2C and B2B communication, but it also works at an employee level. So, it would be wise to give your employees something worthwhile to talk about. Ensuring the culture and values of your company remain alive, motivational and inspirational is a good place to start.

According to a Deloitte survey, 73% of employees who say they work in a Purpose-oriented company are engaged, compared to the 23% of those who don't.[79] Implementing Purpose reviews are therefore just as important as performance reviews. Measuring Purpose helps you check if your people are fully engaged and feel part of the bigger picture, inside and outside of your organization.

---

79 Vaccaro, Adam. "How a Sense of Purpose Boosts Engagement." *Inc.com*. 18 Apr. 2014.
<http://www.inc.com/adam-vaccaro/purpose-employee-engagement.html>.

There are, of course, several challenges in measuring Purpose, given that the current measuring techniques are far from flawless. From our conversations with various Purpose-driven organizations, we identified two main problems with measuring Purpose. One problem is that such surveys are not done on a regular basis. Companies would have a better reflection of their internal cultures if employee surveys were more frequently conducted. The length of 'culture' surveys is another issue. When a survey is too long participants are less likely to be consistent in the way they answer the questions. Similar to measuring NPS (Net Promoter Score, used to measure customer satisfaction and loyalty), our suggestion is to reduce the survey to one single question.

We believe that the *Purpose Review Metric (PRM)* question does the trick. This simple question works because it uniquely measures internal culture components that are directly related to an employee's experience and journey within the organization. The PRM question is measured on a simple 10-point scale and is constructed as follows:

"How inclined are you to recommend your employer to those closest to you, i.e., best friends, relatives, family etc.?"

Figure 17: Purpose Review Metric

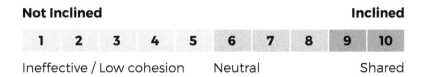

Albeit admittedly simplistic, we come to the conclusion that this single question has the power to elicit the most sincere answers possible. At once the answer to this question offers an indicator of likely performance, discretionary effort, integrity, transparency, clarity and, ultimately, growth. In aggregate, it measures the level of *shared* Purpose within a company's culture and is an indicator how well it is aligned within its broader ecosystem – in particular when contrasted against NPS. If you don't measure NPS in your business, then the question above can simply be replicated outside your business to measure against 'aligned' Purpose.

"How inclined are you to recommend [company X] to those closest to you, i.e., best friends, relatives, family etc.?"

The ultimate goal is to score high in both employee happiness and customer satisfaction. PRM is efficient and works best if asked anonymously and at regular intervals. Forward-thinking companies are acutely aware that measuring shared and aligned Purpose is critical. In fact, W.E. Deming, claims that lack of loyalty toward Purpose is among the top five deadly diseases of American businesses. It goes without saying that this does not only concern American businesses, but companies all around the globe.

Key Performance Indicators (KPIs) for brands, corporations and organizations vary. What they have in common is an alignment with the fundamental goals of what makes a business a business. KPI measurements (which, in this context, includes PRM) are crucial for continued success and should be aligned with *The Guiding Purpose Strategy* at all times.

Five Purpose-oriented KPIs

1. **PRM** - Purpose Review Metric, measuring 'Shared Purpose' within an organization

2. **NPS** - Net Promoter Score, measuring external satisfaction, loyalty and retention, can serve as a proxy for measuring 'Aligned Purpose' within the extended value chain

3. **CAR** - Customer Acquisition Ratio (% of new customers), as an indicator for continued growth

4. **MS** – Market Share (% of market), as a benchmark against competition

5. **EBIT** – Earnings Before Interest & Taxes (operational profit), measuring economic viability

There is a fine line between measuring for the sake of measuring and measuring to manage. If we are to create a better world, then our measurement must take Purpose into account. Or in the words of Bill Gates: "I have been struck again and again by how important measurement is to improving the human condition."

Applying Purpose

Start Focusing and Stop Copying

"Don't try to make a product for everybody,
because that is a product for nobody.
The everybody products are all taken."

Seth Godin
Entrepreneur, Marketing Guru and Writer

Who was the first man to set foot onto the moon? Who was the second... and the third? In July 1969, Neil Armstrong was the first human being to set foot on the moon. Edwin 'Buzz' Aldrin followed only minutes later while Michael Collins kept steering Apollo 11 in the Moon's Orbit. Few of us remember Buzz Aldrin; even fewer recall Michael Collins, although without him the mission could not have been completed. The point here is that focus and positioning are equal. Focus is what drives you from within, while positioning is about occupying a certain space in someone else's mind. If you can't be first, you should re-think your strategy.

You can't be the second Facebook or the next Google. Copying them will not take you anywhere new. What we should notice, however, is that their initial Purpose was not to become large, cool or profitable – taking this road will surely misguide an entrepreneur's journey. Inspired by the need for dealing with the data-complexity of the future, Google's Purpose to

141

'Organize the World's Information' gave the company the thrust and energy to create something new.

There were several search engines before Google and it would be wrong to say that they were the first to occupy that space. The key characteristics of their invention lie in two strategic areas: technology and psychology. It was the first search engine that exclusively focused on the idea of searching. Other search engines displayed information in one big visual clutter, while Google offered one empty search box in the middle of an otherwise white screen. This aesthetic element stemmed from their psychological strategy. Internet users around the world trusted Google Search simply because it did *just that*: search the web.

Facebook's original intention was also not to target the masses. It wasn't the first social network either. Still, it didn't copy the business models of similar networks. Although Facebook wasn't a luxury brand, it began its journey in the top segments, operating first in one of the most elite universities of the US before spreading to other Ivy League colleges. Gradually, it trickled down to other colleges. It then went from students to younger internet users and from there, it conquered businesses and organizations around the globe. The key distinction in Facebook's brand management strategy was the fact that it began from the top of the pyramid, a distinction that created aspiration for the brand. The moral of the story: it's best never to aspire to be what already exists. There's no originality in becoming the second Coca-Cola.

Mark Leiter, CSO of Nielsen, said: "Senior executives in business have grown tired of overpromising and underdelivering and following the do-everything approach, like the famous German *Eierlegende Wollmilchsau* – ('egg-laying-woolly-milk-giving-pig') – vainly trying to do everything for everyone."[80]

Coming back to luxury brands – they tend to be extremely good at positioning. At a macro level, these products are not targeted at everyone to start with. Deliberate eliminators such as price or perception exclude the vast majority of people from the radar screen. Luxury watches priced at $10,000 or above only attract a select group of watch collectors, status-seeking consumers or the 0.1% of the world's population for whom any amount of money is just

---

80 Toppin, Gilbert, and Czerniawska, Fiona *Business Consulting: A Guide to How It Works and How to Make It Work.* London: Profile, 2008.

no issue. Within such a tight, yet competitive market space, positioning is everything. Indeed, it triggers extreme effort on the part of companies seeking to carve out a niche. Take the Hublot "Big Bang $5 million" as another example. It is not only a watch adorned with 1200 stunning diamonds (and costs, as the name indicates, five million), it is also a watch that clearly makes a very bold statement. The Hublot brand is assertive and bold in its positioning, clearly this is not a watch for everybody – even if you have the money. But for the right few, it's just the perfect match.

Applying Purpose requires clarity of positioning to successfully occupy the target audience's minds. We call this space a brand's 3rd place.

Taking 3rd Place

"Meaning leads to profits, not vice versa."

Stuart Crainer and Des Dearlove
British Management Journalists and Business Theorists

Today, it's all about integration. Application Programming Interfaces (APIs) help us integrate quicker and with less friction. If you are a traditional taxi driver, travel agency, hotel, bookseller or asset manager you probably already know what it feels like to live in a 'post-API' world. APIs increasingly connect the world of products and services with the end-consumer without anyone or anything in the middle. This is what is disrupting traditional value chains. This is what fuels the greed and hope of future returns: the assumption that large parts of the middle will be cut out.

You have few strategic choices to emerge as a winner in a post-API world. Either you scale and become so large that you can survive with ever-thinner margins. Or you differentiate and specialize. Whichever strategic context works better for you, the consumers will be less forgiving of imperfect products or brands that overpromise and underdeliver. It's quite Darwinian. The smarter and stronger will survive while the weaker are driven into extinction by an omni-connected consumer who uses opinion as a currency.

The golden nugget is to create a position in the hearts and minds of your customers that is so strong that they will love you no matter what – or almost. As mentioned, Harley-Davidson mastered this feat. The brand has become synonymous with delivering on the promise of life as a journey, including every bit of adventure that goes with it. However, if you were an executive at Harley-Davidson Motor Company in the mid-1920s, you would probably have had quite a different perspective on the future. You would have been stuck in the middle, watching consumers satisfy their needs of transportations with pretty much anything else but a motorcycle. In a sense, Harley was quickly becoming a post-API player of its day.

Harley's strategic choice to escape the middle in the early '30s was powerful, yet pragmatic. They took a bold decision and positioned themselves as a brand that offered a way to spend leisure time away from home, away from work. The idea has worked brilliantly for the last 80 years and is still going strong. In fact, other companies have started adopting this concept, too. Think of Starbucks for example: a great place to socialize, meet people and feel good; or plug in and work for a couple of hours. Not your home, not your office either – it's your third place in a post-API environment.

Today, more than ever, your brand has a direct link to what you have on offer and who buys it (or not) simply because there is less of a buffer. No car dealer is responsible for the defects of your Hyundai, no concierge can butter you up when the room you booked through Airbnb is not quite what you expected. As a brand, you are responsible for the promise and the delivery. Purpose is the glue that holds your brand – staff, suppliers and customers included – together. Creating a 3rd place where everyone in your brand's ecosystem can meet and feel well (physically and mentally) has the potential to give your brand legendary status and yield long-term benefits beyond your wildest imagination.

On the Test of Time

"A nation may be said to consist of its territory, its people, and its laws.
The territory is the only part which is of certain durability.."

Abraham Lincoln
American Politician, Lawyer and President

Operating on Purpose and following *The Guiding Purpose Strategy* is essential to becoming timeless. Timelessness means existing independent of time, outliving trend cycles and establishing a permanent status.

Visionaries and great leaders survive the test of time by staying in sync with their Purpose. If you're looking for a brief moment in the limelight, you are not a member of the Purpose club. *The Guiding Purpose Strategy* is the force behind the notion of heritage and legacy. Preserving heritage is part of the higher Purpose of many traditional luxury brands. People, companies, empires and civilizations come and go, but Purpose-driven brands live on. The progressive pharaohs who led the great Egyptian civilization and built the ancient Egyptian pyramids have long passed away, yet ancient Egypt as a brand is immortal. Thousands of years later, we are still fascinated by Egyptian times: its architects, researchers, archaeologists, historians, scholars, etc.

A timeless brand is one that has mastered the ability of not being tied to a particular phase in time. Such brands have managed to find the utmost profound Know-Why. Many luxury brands do this well. In fact, it is very difficult for a true luxury brand to die. Fabergé, the old Russian fine jewelry brand, was destroyed during its prime due to the Bolshevist revolution. In 1917, the Bolsheviks brought a violent end to Faberge's ateliers, seizing their treasures, closing down production and forcing Fabergé and his family to flee. But Peter Carl Fabergé had already built a timeless brand, which is why after 90 years, the brand was able to revive itself and still persists today.

A. Lange & Söhne, a luxury watch brand, also survived political turmoil. The brand ceased to exist for the longest time until November 9, 1989. The collapse of the Iron Curtain gave Walter Lange the opportunity to bring his family's business back to life. While a brand may vanish from the market, it continues to exist in the collective consciousness of those who cherish it.

Brands have the ability to pass the test of time if they are led by a strong inner Purpose. In their prime, timeless brands touched the hearts and souls of their advocates – the very advocates who will always see to it that their most cherished brands carry on living.

Leadership and Organizational Culture

"Culture eats strategy for breakfast."

Prof. Peter F. Drucker
Austrian-born American Consultant and Author

According a Deloitte Millennial Survey, Millennials overwhelmingly believe (75%) businesses are more focused on their own agendas than helping to improve society.[81] Younger generations will continue to look for meaning beyond profit and demand transparency in 'how we do business.' IBM, for example, uses social Purpose to attract top employees motivated to engage and boost overall performance. It's not about catering to their every whim; it is about helping them make their best contribution to your organization. It's about meeting the challenges and expectations of the Gen Y workforce.

Today's young people are not just younger versions of you – they have different expectations of life and work, and they're shaking things up to induce change. Studies have shown that meaning is so important to people that they actively go about re-crafting their jobs to enhance their sense of

---

81 "Millennial Survey 2017" *Deloitte*. 15 June 2017.
<http://www2.deloitte.com/global/en/pages/about-deloitte/articles/millennialsurvey.html>.

meaningfulness.[82] A new generation of talent has the potential to add energy, innovation and freshness to your organization. But at the same time they can be disruptive, challenging and energy-sapping. In their book called *Real Luxury*, Misha Pinkhasov and Rachna Joshi Nair describe how Generation X and Y view professional life:

> *Generation X and Y (…) no longer feel obliged to aim for the security that a corporate career path provides. To these generations, work looks more like a productive form of play rather than toil. If the baby boomers are thinking about work-life balance, the younger generations are focused on work-life blending where both form a single, pleasurable existence.*[83]

During a Q&A session at Yale University, Eric Schmidt, former CEO of Google, said: "One of the things you learn about decision-making is that you don't want a single person making the decision, you want groups making decisions and you want those groups to be making decision under the principle of 'we will make the best decision not the consensus decision.' […] We [at Google] will sit there and debate until everyone says that's the best idea as opposed to warring consensus arguments." Fostering an open dialogue that encourages inclusive decisions requires more than an open attitude and a mindset that can think beyond ego. It requires a carefully crafted mix of people, behavior and vision. The prefix to operating in such a mode is a culture of excellence based on values and ambition – which in turn is, of course, intrinsically linked to the very reason why we exist.

How should a leader who is trying to create a strong culture within the organization look at this concept? Organizational culture can only be cultivated and maintained if all acknowledge the fact that the best result would come from everyone in the group doing what is best for himself or herself and the group. So, then, what is the most optimal way of achieving this as a leader? The answer is hidden in plain sight: by making the transition to become Purpose-

---

82 "What Makes Work Meaningful – Or Meaningless." *MIT Sloan Management Review*. <http://sloanreview.mit.edu/article/what-makes-work-meaningful-or-meaningless/?utm_medium=social&utm_source=twitter&utm_campaign=featjune16>.
83 Pinkhasov, Misha, and Nair, Rachna Joshi. *Real Luxury: How Luxury Brands Can Create Value for the Long Term*. Basingstoke: Palgrave Macmillan, 2014.

led. Research by IMD and Burson Marsteller, "provides strong evidence that leadership is a strong and consistent predictor of authentic corporate Purpose, explaining almost 50% of the variance in perceptions of authenticity."[84]

Becoming a Purpose-led brand and organization is not a mathematical issue – it's a geometrical one. Euclid, often referred to as the 'Father of Geometry,' was an ancient Greek intellectual who created an axiomatic system worth remembering. Euclid stated that if two things are equal to the same thing, they are equal to each other. If all the individuals within a company (including the leadership) can be equal to the brand rather than the leader or the CEO, they would all be equal to each other. A strong set of arguments can't unite people, but a strong philosophy can. A mathematical model may be able to connect individuals but a geometrical model can unify them. In other words, a successful company can't do what a successful brand can, namely bond teams together. It represents a uniting canvas for shared and aligned Purpose.

Leonid Matsih, philosopher and theologian, stated in one of his lectures that rituals help us sense the meaning of life. Activities with ritualistic value include drawing, meditating, dancing, creative writing, playing a musical instrument and singing. We are not suggesting that you implement a Walmart-style 'morning chant' with your staff to kick off your daily business routine. But if you are PricewaterhouseCoopers and your Purpose is '*To build trust in society and solve important problems,*'[85] then creating a trustworthy working environment is key. Subtle, institutionalized rituals such as five-minute insight-sharing sessions every morning for instance can help create an environment of stimulation.

More than anyone, business leaders and senior management are responsible for aligning employees with an overarching Purpose. A Deloitte survey found that 47% of executives strongly agree that they can identify with their company's Purpose, compared with 30% of employees.[86] Shared and aligned Purpose is a must-have. It provides employees with a sense of belonging

---

84 "Power Of Purpose." *Power Of Purpose*. <http://powerofpurpose.burson-marsteller.com/wp-content/uploads/2015/04/BM_IMD_REPORT-How-Authentic-is-your-Corporate-Purpose.pdf>

85 PwC Purpose Statement, <https://www.pwc.co.uk/who-we-are/corporate-sustainability/our-purpose.html>

86 Vaccaro, Adam. "How a Sense of Purpose Boosts Engagement." *Inc.com*. 18 Apr. 2014. <http://www.inc.com/adam-vaccaro/purpose-employee-engagement.html>.

and helps them understand their role within the bigger picture. Research conducted by McKinsey confirms that meaning drives higher workplace productivity and in turn growth and profit.[87] So how then does Purpose propel growth?

87 Keller, Susie Cranston and Scott. "Increasing the 'meaning Quotient' of Work." *McKinsey & Company.*
<http://www.mckinsey.com/business-functions/organization/our-insights/increasing-the-meaning-quotient-of-work>.

How Purpose Propels Growth

"Without continual growth and progress,
such words as improvement, achievement,
and success have no meaning."

Benjamin Franklin
Polymath, Diplomat and one of the
Founding Fathers of the US

Shares of meaningful companies have gone up approximately 600% on a 10-year average.[88] There is a growing tendency of both large and small organizations to prioritize the inner Know-Why to navigate in the new economic environment of the 21st century. More and more large companies are joining the Purpose-led revolution.

The Ernst & Young Beacon Institute, which was launched at the 2015 World Economic Forum in Davos, joined forces with the Saïd Business School at the University of Oxford and Harvard Business Review Analytic Services to begin transforming businesses through the principle of Purpose. According to their research, 87% of 474 global executives believe companies perform best in the long-term if their Purpose goes beyond the bottom line of financial

---

88 Bains, Gurnek. *Meaning Inc.: The Blueprint for Business Success in the 21st Century.* London: Profile, 2006.

results.[89] All challenges related to trust, leadership, employee engagement, efficiency, branding, sustainability, entrepreneurship and innovation are being reoriented with one powerful component that can hold the entire temple of commerce together – Purpose.

One of the most common mistakes companies make is to confuse Purpose with corporate social responsibility (CSR). Yes, every Purpose-driven enterprise is sustainable, ethical and socially responsible, however, not every business with a CSR section in its annual report is a meaningful, Purpose-led business. In 1987, the *Brundtland Report* defined sustainability in business as "development that meets the needs of the present without compromising the ability of future generations to meet their own needs."[90]

Sustainability, laterally speaking, is divided into three branches – environmental, social and economic. The environmental side is obviously about the ecological health of our planet, the social side is about the overall wellbeing of employees within the company and its supply chains and, finally, the economic side is about monetary profit. What is truly interesting is that whilst there is quite a lot of media coverage about the first two elements, there is very little on the economic impact. We believe that without a strong inner Purpose at work, increasing revenue and profit will be harder to achieve in the future. Indeed, Purpose and profits are increasingly intertwined.

In order to fully comprehend the blend of making profits and helping society, it is useful to look at it from a personal perspective. If you, as an individual, are trying to achieve self-actualization by working on yourself for yourself, you are least likely to achieve it since it is a rather an egotistical aim. However, if you are trying to develop yourself to be a better husband or a better corporate partner, it is a different story. This means you are improving for yourself and for others. This approach doesn't just emphasize the idea of serving. Rather, it provides the model whereby transforming and improving yourself first, will allow you to give back. So, in other words, Purpose is just as much about the impact on the lives of the founder, the chairman, the board

---

89 Bitti, Mary Teresa. "Why Starbucks CEO Howard Schultz Is Looking beyond Profits to a Purpose-led Strategy." *Financial Post.* 05 June 2015. <http://business.financialpost.com/entrepreneur/why-starbucks-ceo-howard-schultz-is-looking-beyond-profits-to-a-purpose-led-strategy>.
90 "Topic." *International Institute for Sustainable Development.* <http://www.iisd.org/topic/sustainable-development>.

of directors, and the employees as it is about the impact on customers, linking back to our concept of shared and aligned Purpose.

The idea of shared and aligned Purpose should never be perceived as an image of soldiers standing in artificially symmetrical order. It is to be pictured as the natural order of the red seeds inside a pomegranate. The positioning of each seed is aesthetically unique, fine-tuned, and organic. Purpose is the source of energy that sets things in motion. It drives the organization or the individual to prosperity with its force of motivation and aspiration. Employees of Purpose-driven organizations go the extra mile because it is motivating to be able contribute to meaning beyond their paycheck.

Think of the new educational tech company Coursera. It doesn't merely promise to democratize education; it actually delivers it. They make courses from the most prestigious universities around the world accessible no matter where you reside. Their core Purpose is genuine and hidden within their mission statement of 'Providing universal access to the world's best education.' It's not quite as aptly worded as we would want it to be, but it is meaningful in that it directly addresses the global challenges of education. As UNESCO reports, the number of out-of-school children is on the rise from 124 million in 2013.[91] Coursera's overarching Purpose transcends money and gives the brand a meaning with which employees, students and stakeholders alike can whole-heartedly identify.

Purpose is not only a key corporate economic booster. It is also important on an individual level. One of the greatest aspects of Purpose is its capacity to advance intuition by encouraging clear introspection. A problem among professionals, entrepreneurs and leaders is that they perceive Purpose as something extrinsic. This train of thought leads to the failure of aligning intention with action. Taking the next step is pointless when your intentions are not clear. Purpose is often conflated with aims, goals, objectives etc. However, a *Guiding Purpose Strategy* is of absolute intrinsic value. It is the discovery of the Know-Why, and its intuition helps you uncover it.

---

91 World Bank *Twitter*. 30 Oct. 2015. <https://twitter.com/WorldBank/status/660010976650113024>.

Making it Happen

Conquering Time

"Everything has been figured out, except how to live."

Jean-Paul Sartre
French Existentialist

We live in times of acceleration. Technology moves faster than most of us can grasp and constant change is the new norm. Yet, since the very beginning of recorded history the notion of time has always been the one thing in this world that no one can fully conquer. Nobody has been able to capture 25 hours in a day or nine days in a week. However, it doesn't take being a great analyst to see that some perceive and use their time significantly better than others.

Why do some of the busiest people seem to use time significantly better than others? Purpose-driven professionals, entrepreneurs and leaders use their time better because they adopt a certain way of thinking in regards to the notion of time. As Leonardo da Vinci once stated: "Time stays long enough for anyone who will use it." Having this mindset means, first of all, respecting and valuing one's own time. Embedding a Purpose-driven strategy is not a quick win – it will take good time.

People have the habit of asking "How much time do I have?" But maybe that's not the right question to ask to start with. Perhaps, asking the opposite would be more appropriate: "How much of me does time have?" – time can consume us if we do not know how to master it.

Here is a familiar example: you go to your inbox to see if you have received the email you have been waiting for. Even though this can be done in a matter of seconds, you get distracted and end up watching a 12-minute 'short' video, all whilst a friend pings over a nice but unimportant WhatsApp message – and you decide to take a look and reply. Before you know it, 30 minutes have passed instead of the 30 seconds it should have taken to check on that email. Procrastination works in similar ways, picking the easy things first, delaying the important stuff until we eventually have no other option than to tackle it.

The reason behind such time-wasting behavior is strongly linked to attention and time. A recent study by Microsoft found that a digital lifestyle has made it more difficult for us to stay focused, with the human attention span shortening from 12 seconds to eight seconds in less than a decade.[92] Being focused and determined on one or several prespecified things is the way to avoid distraction and wasting time.

Time is perceived in different ways in different business cultures but all agree on one thing: time changes everything and the only thing that doesn't change is change itself.

There are two fundamental ways of looking at how time is spent:

1. As time passes, value is lost
2. As time passes, value increases

Some people grow weaker and more passive as they get older, while others get wiser and more important with age. What about brands? Michael Eisner, former CEO of The Walt Disney Company, offers the perfect answer: "A brand is a living entity – and it is enriched or undermined cumulatively over time, the product of a thousand small gestures."

While many business leaders say one should spend *more* time on self-

---

92 Borreli, Lizette. "Why A Goldfish Probably Has A Better Attention Span Than You." *Medical Daily.* 14 May 2015. <http://www.medicaldaily.com/human-attention-span-shortens-8-seconds-due-digital-technology-3-ways-stay-focused-333474>.

development, Peter Drucker, the legendary management consultant and author, used to say you should "organize your self-development". The two approaches are very different. Organizing does not mean doing more of the same thing but structuring it in an optimum way. What is the simplest way of structuring and organizing self-development? And how can we use it to help us activate the power of Purpose?

To conquer time, three important angles have to complement each other: *MeTime*, *SocialTime* and *ProductiveTime*. The latter is directly linked to 'what we do' and 'how to do it.' It seems only logical then to spend enough time thinking about 'why we do what we do' before focusing on making the most out of it.

Figure 18: The Triangle of Time

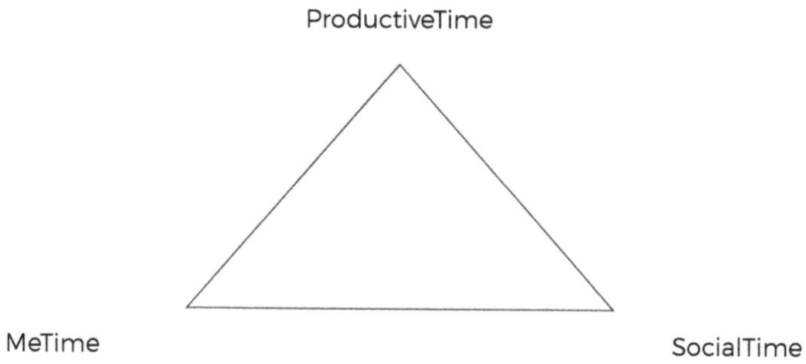

ProductiveTime

MeTime   SocialTime

MeTime

There is a series of things that we do during the week that are so basic that we hardly think about them. But what if we redefined activities such as walking the dog or watering the plants as *MeTime*? We would then perceive these activities as stimulating tasks to foster contemplation, instead of mere banal responsibilities. Making most of *MeTime* requires a conscious reflection on what to do with the time for oneself. Here are a few tips to get started:

Designate a portion of the day to contemplate and plan
This is taking the time to contemplate specific aspects of your life that require finding solutions, analyzing for the short- or mid-term, thinking about goals, making a plan B, etc.

Designate a portion of the day to dream

This is when the doors of perception are wide open and you allow your limitless imagination to float freely; thinking is as broad as vast oceans, the tallest mountains and widest deserts, a moment of reflection in which everything becomes possible.

Designate a portion of the day to meditate

There is a certain state of being, a level above all levels that words cannot reach nor teach. Or in timeless words of Rumi, the 13th-century Sufi philosopher and jurist: "Out beyond ideas of wrong doing and right doing, there is a field. I'll meet you there. When the soul lies down in that grass, the world is too full to talk about."

Me Time also includes spending time on social or cultural entertainment, leisure activities and hobbies, whether they are done collectively or individually. The way you structure your time such activities is crucial. Throughout history, humanity has witnessed countless discoveries and inventions that changed the course of history. More often than not such monumental ideas were born during the trivialities of *Me Time* – taking a shower, playing a violin, daydreaming, etc.

During his speech at the Stanford Graduate School of Business, Sir James Wolfensohn, the ninth President of the World Bank, spoke of spending one's time:

> *"If there is one thing that I would as a generality say to you, it is that if it is possible for you, in whatever you are doing to engage yourself in things other than the straight business course, you will find that not only does it enrich your life, but the truth of the matter is that it'll enrich your business."*[93]

Spending time is perceived as an investment. The link between attention and time is always something to keep in mind. Those that don't value this notion run the risk of not being able to grasp the intricacies of governing time.

---

93 Stanfordbusiness. "Former World Bank President: Big Shift Coming." *YouTube*. 29 Jan. 2010.
<https://www.youtube.com/watch?v=6a0zhc1y_Ns>

SocialTime

SocialTime is not (only) about being on Snapchat or Facebook. By *SocialTime* we mean spending time with friends, family or colleagues at the coffee machine at work. It refers to the time spent not directly producing or solving work problems. Often a static picture of the traditional family is what commonly comes to mind when we think about *SocialTime*. However, we need to be careful about what we mean by this. According to Gillian Hampsen-Thompson, Professor of Education at the University of Sussex, "The 'traditional family' is something of a post-war invention – and the idealism that surrounds it is seriously flawed. Families are complex and fluid units."[94] One needs to acknowledge the fact that a family is not a static institution and that trying to uphold the engineered image of a perfect family is consuming. The same goes for friends. The goal is to find an environment where we can detach from routine and enjoy the richness of unconstrained emotions, lean on a friend's shoulder and most importantly, learn and grow. It is being able to know where family, friends and social activity fit in terms of our inner value system, so we can get the most out of *SocialTime*.

If we manage to balance *MeTime*, *SocialTime* and *ProductiveTime* we move ourselves into pole position to successfully align with our inner Purpose. Without a doubt, *ProductiveTime* is where most issues arise; either because we don't have enough time to do it all or simply because we are not good enough at how we do what we do. Since we spend most of our working lives 'doing' or what we call *ProductiveTime*, this dominant area also affects our *MeTime* and *SocialTime*.

The following chapter lists a collection of tested ideas and techniques to help master the domain of *ProductiveTime*.[95]

---

94 Hampden-Thompson, Gillian. "Stable Families, Not 'traditional' Ones, Key to Children's Education Success." *The Conversation.* 18 June 2017. <http://theconversation.com/stable-families-not-traditional-ones-key-to-childrens-education-success-36158>.
95 Source: personal collection and consolidation of experiences, productivity literate, *The 4-Hour Workweek* by Tim Ferris, *Getting Things Done* by David Allen, *The Power of Habit* by Charles Duhigg, *Zero to One* by Peter Thiels, others.

Productivity Mantra

*"We are what we repeatedly do.
Excellence, then, is not an act, but a habit."*

Aristotle
Greek Polymath

Stop multitasking.
Computers are made for multitasking. Humans operate better when focusing on one task at a time. We can derive a great deal of power from developing a laser focus on a particular task at hand. Doing one thing at a time, doing it well and doing it right the first time.

Eliminate distractions.
Convenience is the mother of distraction, so make it difficult to satisfy temptations. Shut down the browser, leave your phone behind, close the door or move to a different room to get stuff done.

Focus your meetings.
People generally don't need as much time as they request – give them half of the time they ask for. This forces everyone to be brief, clear and to the point. This is efficiency, without being unkind.

Create productivity rituals.

Prioritize one key task to accomplish per day. Checking emails in the afternoon helps you reserve the peak energy hours of your mornings for your best work. Work in 90-minute intervals with short breaks. Structure your day and follow a rhythm.

Write a Stop-Doing list.

Every productive person obsessively sets To-Do lists. But the experts also record what they commit not to do.

Get up earlier.

Use your morning to seize the day: mind over mattress.

Exercise.

Exercise is energizing and makes us healthier. Additionally, exercise can improve our mood for up to 12 hours after we work out. Work out for at least 20 minutes a day. Feel better. Be smarter. Be less stressed. Have a more productive day.

Use your mind for thinking, not remembering.

The best way to have a good idea is to have a lot of ideas. Note them down when they are fresh, and use active thinking time later to develop or discard them. Thinking time shouldn't be something to get around to when you get a chance. Schedule two hours of *Me Time* each Tuesday morning.

Make technology your friend.

There's a wealth of programs to help increase productivity: Evernote to keep track of tasks, lists and things to read-later, Dropbox to store files, WebEx to host webinars, Hootsuite to schedule social media posts and so on.

Just Say No.

Protect your time – the one asset no one can afford to waste. Say 'no' at least as often as you say yes. You can be polite while protecting time. And remember, scarcity yields desirability.

Get enough sleep.
Most of us constantly have our fingers on the fast-forward button, when we really need to hit pause for a while. You can only carry on not sleeping enough for a while before it catches up with you.

Automate.
Write down your daily routine, from getting up, to exercising, to what to wear and eat, to when you go to bed. Then follow through. No rule without exceptions, but structure helps us focus our energy on the important things. Productivity is not about luck. It's about devotion.

Use the commute.
If you commute for 30 minutes each way every day use that time to listen to great audiobooks or catch up on social media when in a train.

Live in the now.
Practice active listening, pay attention and remain focused when interacting with people at work and at home. Attention is reciprocal.

Disconnect.
Don't be so available to everyone. Stop the 24/7 connectivity urge. Turn off your devices and think, create, plan and write. Zero interruptions. Pure focus. Massive results.

Branding Thyself

"There were lots of things that could drive a man mad,
especially if he didn't have the resolution,
the Purpose, required for learning;
but when a man had a clear, unbending intent,
feelings were in no way a hindrance,
for he was capable of controlling them."

Don Juan
Yaqui Shaman

Some call it self-marketing, others call it personal branding. The notion of branding ourselves is largely misunderstood. We must first avoid the confusing terms of self-marketing or personal branding. A more useful term is perhaps 'branding thyself.' Notice that we intentionally change it from *self* to *thyself* in order to emphasize that this is based on your world within. Why is branding thyself becoming ever more crucial? What are the intricate nuances of branding thyself in the most effective way?

In times of increased transparency and exposure, the idea of creating one's own brand to underpin a particular value proposition, an area of expertise and so on is no longer an act of magic. Applying the same tested and tried frameworks that help corporates define, refine, position and communicate their brands successfully is available to any individual aiming to propel his or her own brand into the future. The frameworks outlined in the previous chapter *'The GPS Framework'* work just as well for individuals.

However, putting up a profile on LinkedIn and writing a few blog posts is not enough. Making it all look nice is not that complex. Sticking it on a good website with good visual differentiation is a bit trickier, but still nothing out of the ordinary. The biggest struggle is to know and be clear about who you really are, not who you want to be.

When we analyze the creation of effective value systems that lead to outstanding examples of branding thyself, we find that in this context 'the origin' is the message. On an individual 'branding' level, Purpose is the message. Since each of us on this planet has something unique within, the number of 'personal brands' that can potentially be built is astronomical. Branding thyself is becoming more important than ever, predominantly because we are entering the age of the supreme network and radical transparency, a world in which the opinion economy is not just part of the economy – it *is* the economy.

Within the global ecosystem of opinions it is possible to develop a personal philosophy and become the great architect of your innate universe with the aim to create an infinite *Youniverse*. Remember that people are no longer going to be satisfied with your outer appearance. Appearance is not out of the equation but today it definitely is no longer enough for *branding thyself.* The more meaningful your cosmos within, the more essential your essence is to the audience. Generation Y and beyond wants to see your Know-Why. Getting your professional makeup done and sharing cute photos on social media is not enough. It lacks Purpose. You must also be photogenic from within. Think of the many examples of the luxury brands we cited in this book. Many share key elements of their internal cultures, their higher Purpose and some of their secret know-how etc. Turning oneself inside out is about revealing what really goes on behind the scenes and why. The inner cult that is derived from your inner Purpose manifests a culture to the outer world, which can be brought to life through the discipline of brand management. Creating a profile, a website, a video and so on is only going to be consistent and integral if it reflects your inner self.

Saying something in an *outro*spective way rather than in an introspective way can be perceived as copying or paraphrasing. In other words, target audiences wouldn't perceive it as sincere or original. What can be accepted as genuinely new and legitimate is the message that comes from the inner-why.

For example, take Sir Richard Branson, founder of the Virgin Group. He is incredibly good at branding himself. Why? Because he has absolute clarity on his Purpose in life. Sir Richard Branson is a visionary who has a value set that is vividly embedded within his brand. He became a business magnate because he always stayed true to his higher Purpose within of 'Changing business for good.' He has never forgotten this and he never hesitates to project it onto the outer world. It is worth visiting Virgin's website to appreciate how deeply Richard Branson believes in the power of Purpose.[96]

Elon Musk, CEO and product architect of Tesla Motors is also one of the entrepreneurs who has mastered the mechanics of branding thyself rather than merely dwelling in lavish self-promotion. He runs Tesla Inc., SpaceX, SolarCity – all at once. It is not incidental that Elon Musk devotes so much of his time brand managing his internal self. As a serial entrepreneur, the time invested in branding the world within is not time lost but time spent intelligently.

The complexity of choice and the growing number of communication channels underlines how branding thyself will function as an enabler to unleash the power of personal Purpose in the years ahead. We believe that self-branding will form part of the core skills people need to develop in the next 25 years. In a world where the consumer[97] has the power, having the ability to market oneself is key. Let not your short-term interests, but your innate Purpose be your guiding principle.

---

96 <https://www.virgin.com/richard-branson/power-purpose>
97 Please note, we use the term 'consumer' very broadly here; this can also be understood as prospects, co-workers, recruiters and any other audience of relevance.

Cultivating the Culture of the Self

"It is in constantly paying attention to oneself that one assures one's salvation."

Gaius Musonius Rufus
Roman Stoic Philosopher

People, countries, industries and *some* brands have culture. However, culture does not have to be a collective phenomenon only. Some individuals do have a private inner culture within, which they build throughout their lifetime. In ancient times, the Greek and Roman philosophers called it 'the culture of the self.' Unlike animals, human beings are conscious, thinking beings. Therefore, the need for cultivating a culture of the self is a natural need. Yet, few succeed at it. Epictetus, the ancient Stoic philosopher, once said: "Men are this unique kind of beings on earth who have to take care of themselves. Nature has provided animals with everything they need, humans don't have the same natural equipment, but we must understand that the necessity of taking care of ourselves is also a supplementary gift, which has been bestowed."

So what's the benefit of creating an individual culture? Why do decision-makers, managers, marketers or anyone trying to master any craft need to keep developing and cultivating this culture of the self?

Inner culture provides a larger space for the times when the world outside seems too limiting. Inner culture offers us a kind of inner dynamo that contributes to personal skills such as intuition, introspection, imagination, etc. It is about having the ability to create your own legend about life itself. It is not a list of values about virtue, ethics and righteousness – these are too abstract to be intuitive. Rather, this is about constructing a *system* of values. The culture of the self is a great meaning system that helps maintain the *multiple personality order*. But, above all, it is about having a Purpose in one's life, providing guidance during the stormy adventures throughout life's journey.

Developing a culture of the self requires one to be concerned with oneself for the sake of others and also to be concerned with oneself for oneself. Caring for oneself is not a new concept. Greek and Roman philosophers called it *epimeleia heautou* (Greek for 'care of self') and it was one of the main principles of ethics, one of the main rules for the art of living for an entire millennium. One should take into account that it is never too early and never too late to occupy oneself with one's true essence, with one's true self. Gaius Musonius Rufus, a Roman Stoic philosopher of the 1st century stated: "It is in the act of constantly paying attention to oneself that one assures one's salvation."

The 20th-century French philosopher and philologist Michel Foucault gave a triumphant lecture at UC Berkeley on the culture of the self in 1983. During this lecture he said: "What was the most important moral principle, the most characteristic in ancient philosophy? The answer, which comes immediately to mind, is not *epimeleia heautou* ('care of the self') but, as you know, *gnōthi seauton*, which is, 'know thyself'". Perhaps the Western historical and philosophical tradition has somehow overrated the importance of the 'know yourself.' In the Far East there are teachings that explain how being *too* aware of your self doesn't help in taking care of yourself. Cultivating the culture of the self requires conscious self-mastery.

The Future of Personal Mastery

"You should view the world as a conspiracy
run by a very closely-knit group of nearly omnipotent people,
and you should think of those people as yourself and your friends."

Robert Anton Wilson
Futurist and Writer

What will the future practitioners of cultivating the self be doing? In which direction is this practice headed? As social scientists continue making advancements in fields such as anthropology, neuroscience, psychology, behavioral economics, etc., self-development is advancing as well.

Over materialism, essentialism will prevail. All marketing and branding strategies, all communication from the individual to the collective will include the essential true self, for it will be viewed as the most authentic asset. It will be accepted as the best means of contact and bonding. In the ancient times 'the way of living' was a significant philosophical matter. Then came the meaning of life or the Purpose of life. Both, however, had the same underlying motivation, which was to find the best way to develop the culture of the self, to take care and fine-tune oneself. Because deciding to take care of your true self is a decision that is in the interest of all.

From this perspective, we believe that understanding and consciously applying a *Guiding Purpose Strategy* is most essential. Today, we are already at a stage where it has been operationally proven that brand essence or the inner self can be embellished by finding and articulating Purpose. Over the course of our industrial history, luxury brands have demonstrated how enriching a clearly articulated inner self can become. The existential Know-Why is already becoming the new operational know-how. Our children and grandchildren will advance *The Guiding Purpose Strategy* even further. Cultivating the self will be integrated into our lifestyles to the extent that *The Guiding Purpose Strategy* will encompass one's private, social and business life.

As Buckminster Fuller would agree, the children of the future will do what needs to be done, as they will be aware of the fact that that's how the universe designed itself. We firmly believe that people will increasingly use tools such as applying a *Guiding Purpose Strategy* to change the world for the better. The leaders of the future will use their inner Know-Why to adapt the world to them rather than adapting themselves to a limited pre-defined worldview.

True Purpose that radiates from within cannot be separated from personal mastery of the inner self. As brand makers, business builders and individuals, the only way forward is not just to pass on what we have built. We must take advantage of our ability and know-how to advance the Know-Why for generations to come.

The Last Word

Wanderer Above the Mist
Caspar David Friedrich, 1818

Like a child's first visit to a dazzling circus
An exciting feeling you cannot purchase
Discovering this deep inner Purpose
Oh, being aware of its guiding service

To articulate it and bring it to surface
To record it poetically in endless verses
To the point when we are left wordless
To, finally, escape all cycles and circuits

One inner cult of yours,
From which all culture will derive
A vast blue ocean of fortune
Patiently waiting for you to dive
Hidden within, as an intuitive drive
An inner voice of growth, of being alive
To navigate upwards, not to merely survive
Transcending cycles, to finally thrive!

By Tofig Husein-zadeh

We cannot but hope that the consolidated words, expertise, frameworks and wisdom of great minds both past and present have achieved at least one thing: to help you, the reader to advance your thinking, to stimulate your mind, your understanding and your ambition to use the power of Purpose to bring about positive change.

It is our deepest hope that meaningfulness will penetrate to change brands, organizations and their leaders and people generally for the better.

Onwards and Upwards!

Notes

"The Guiding Purpose Strategy provides inspiring insights on how to navigate for professional and personal success through the lens of 21st century brand management."

Moira Clark, Professor of Strategic Marketing, Henley Business School

"You can't get better than a 'been-there-done-that' global expert taking the time to reflect on his experiences and share his wisdom. Markus is one of the best, and this book is a must read for anyone wanting to know about the future of brand management."

Graeme Codrington, Futurist & CEO, TomorrowToday Global

"One fresh and fascinating read in contemporary brand management."

Dil Sidhu, Associate Dean, Executive Education, Columbia Business School

"The Guiding Purpose Strategy is wonderfully stimulating, practical and in many ways a modern technique to build and unleash brand performance."

Dr Sepehr Tarverdian, CEO Hamayesh Farazan

"Focus, clarity and direction are priceless when it comes to determining factors for successful entrepreneurship. The Guiding Purpose Strategy is a great way to get all of this and more."

Willi Helbling, CEO Business Professionals Network (NGO)

The Authors

Markus Kramer is a partner at Brand Affairs, a consulting agency specializing in advising boards and executives on all aspects of strategic positioning and brand management. Kramer has worked with brands such as Harley-Davidson, Aston Martin, Ferrari, international banks, governments, NGOs, startups and many more. He is a visiting Associate Professor in Brand Management at Cass Business School in London and a recognized thought leader in the fast-paced world of cutting edge brand management. Kramer holds degrees in Marketing & Brand Management from the University of California at Berkeley and an MBA from the University of Oxford.

Tofig Husein-zadeh is a brand strategist, business writer, psychographics researcher, translator and speaker. A former writer for Harvard Business Review, his articles about luxury brand management have been published by The Brand Age and Campaign. Husein-zadeh is the founder of the biannual print magazine The Intelligentsia.